FINDING
CANADIAN
FACTS
FAST

FINDING
CANADIAN
FACTS
FAST

STEPHEN OVERBURY

McGraw-Hill Ryerson
Toronto   Montreal

FINDING CANADIAN FACTS FAST

First published in 1989 by
McGraw-Hill Ryerson Limited
330 Progress Avenue
Scarborough, Ontario M1P 2Z5

Design by Christopher Griffin

1234567890 M 8765432109

CANADIAN CATALOGUING IN PUBLICATION DATA
   Overbury, Stephen
      Finding Canadian facts fast

[2nd ed.]
ISBN 0-07-549695-X

1. Research – Methodology – Handbooks, manuals, etc.
2. Information services – Canada.   I. Title.

Q180.55.M4092 1989   001.4'2   C89-093370-7

Printed and bound in Canada

For Jennifer and Kristina

Contents

Preface

The nice thing about writing a book such as this is the opportunity to work on a second edition. *Finding Canadian Facts Fast* has been changed in two significant ways. The first change previous readers will recognize is the introduction of new material: an excellent summary of telephone techniques now appears in Chapter One; a new section on tracing ancestors is in Chapter Nine; there is an expanded section on using on-line computer searches in Chapter Twelve; and new pages appear for the first time on the use of school libraries (for the benefit of younger readers), also in Chapter Twelve.

The second change, and an inevitable one with this kind of material, is the updating of titles, names and addresses in Part Two of the book. The idea behind the inclusion of source material is to offer a sense of what is out there, to stimulate the researcher's appetite. To attempt anything else would be futile as there are thousands of reference books and other avenues which itemize an endless array of Canadian sources.

Naturally, some of the sources listed will change over the years. If you have any questions or comments please write to me at: Post Office Box 951, Station Q, Toronto, Ontario M4T 2P1.

Acknowledgements

This book would not have been written without the generous support and encouragement of many people. They are listed here with the titles they held either when interviewed for the first edition in 1984 or at the time this second edition was being written.

A special thanks to Salem Alaton, a reporter with the *Globe and Mail*, who helped me immensely with editing and consulting services throughout the project.

I also owe a special thanks to my clients and to students who have attended my courses and seminars. These students, hundreds of them, came from many different professional backgrounds and, with their great variety of questions, helped to shape the content of this book. The courses and seminars were presented at these educational institutions: Concordia University, Humber College, Ryerson Polytechnical Institute, Seneca College, University of Toronto, and the University of Western Ontario. I also presented seminars for many trade unions, including the Amalgamated Transit Union, the Ontario Public Service Employees Union, the United Auto Workers (now the Canadian Auto Workers), and the United Steelworkers of America. Seminars were also presented at the Canadian Broadcasting Corporation Producer's Training Program. Many seminars were also offered to major businesses in different industries from coast to coast.

Naturally, many "information specialists" shared the secrets of their trade by consenting to long interviews and in so

doing took the mystery out of research. Those who were helpful for Part One of this bok were: Professor of History J.M.S.
Careless of the University of Toronto; Frank Drea, a former
cabinet minister with the Ontario government; novelist
Timothy Findley; Dr. Louis Siminovitch, Director of Research
at Mount Sinai Hospital in Toronto; Calvin Hill of the detective
agency Intertel; Brian Land of the Ontario Government's
Legislative Library; Hugh P. MacMillan of the Public Archives
of Ontario; Paul McLaughlin author of *Asking Questions: The
Art of the Media Interview*; Julian Porter, a Toronto attorney;
Arthur R. Roberts, a police trainer, and John Zaritsky, a television producer with the CBC.

For Part Two, the following people were helpful with the
chapter on using libraries: Beryl L. Anderson and Paul Otto
of the Library Documentation Centre, National Library of
Canada; Robert Gibson, President of Micromedia Limited;
Susan Klement, an award-winning Toronto librarian; librarians Brian Land and Janet Moore; Roger J. Smith, Chairman of
the School Librarianship Department, Faculty of Education,
University of Toronto, who wrote the portion of the book dealing with school libraries; and Ulla de Stricker of Micromedia
Limited.

I was assisted in the chapter on local government sources by
Barbara G. Caplan of the City of Toronto Clerk's Department;
Elizabeth Cuthbertson of the City of Toronto archives; Bob
Halifax of the City of Toronto Central Records Department;
Bruce Macnaughton of the Ontario Ministry of Municipal
Affairs and Housing; and Michael John Smither of Municipal
World Incorporated.

The following people were very helpful in the researching of
provincial government sources: Wayne Carr of the Ontario
Ministry of Consumer and Commercial Relations; James C.
Crawford, an attorney in Newmarket, Ontario, who specializes
in real estate; Gordon Dodds, Chief of Government Records for
the Province of Manitoba; Allen Doppelt of the Ontario Ministry of Consumer and Commercial Relations; Janet Globe,
author of *Title Searching in Ontario* (Butterworths of Toronto,
1982); J.L. Haughey, a land registrar for the City of Toronto;
John-Paul Haward, Land Registrar for Metropolitan Toronto;
Irvin Lutsky of the Investment Dealers' Association of Canada;
Pierre Morin, Direction générale de l'administration et des
enterprises, Gouvernement du Québec; Julian Sher, a Mont-
real-based journalist; Norman Sterling, a Member of Parlia-

ment for Ontario; Linda Stortz of Micromedia Limited, and Carl Vervoort of the Ontario Ministry of Transportation and Communications.

My thanks to the following for their assistance with federal government sources: the staff at Consumer and Corporate Affairs Canada; Michael Dagg, a freelance researcher, based in Ottawa; Tom Fournier of Labour Canada's Bureau of Labour Information; Raulet Gaudet, an Ottawa-based journalist with Radio-Canada International; Lorne J. Kenney and Nicole Lemay of the Bureau of Labour Information; Netta Maskell of the Canada Service Bureau Program, and Lionel Sauvé of the Canadian Government Publishing Centre in Ottawa. I would also like to thank Heather Mitchell, a Toronto attorney, and Murray Rankin of the Faculty of Law, University of Victoria, who are co-authors of *Using the Access to Information Act* (Self-Counsel Press).

In preparing the chapter on court records, I was assisted by David A. Avery of the Ontario Ministry of the Attorney General; Warren J. Dunlop of the Supreme Court of Ontario; Harold J. Levy, author of *A Reporter's Guide To Canada's Criminal Justice System* (Canadian Bar Foundation); James Moore of the federal Department of Justice, and Stuart M. Robertson, a Toronto attorney and author of *Courts and the Media* (Butterworths of Toronto, 1981).

Other people who assisted me include: the staff of the Archives of Labor and Urban Affairs at the Walter P. Reuther Library, Wayne State University (where, believe it or not, I obtained background information on Frank Drea!); Donald Armitage of Dun and Bradstreet International; Victor Brunka; Suzanna Buenaventura who patiently typed large chunks of the second edition; Michael Dufault, a Toronto-based freelance editor; the staff of the Faculty of Library Science at the University of Toronto; Sean Fernando of A.B.C. Property and Liens Reports, Toronto; Kelly C.J. LaBrash of Canadian Protection Services Limited, Toronto, and veteran journalist Bob Reguly.

How to Use This Book

In the first edition of *Finding Canadian Facts Fast* I wrote that there is no such thing as information you can't access. The CBC's "Morningside" radio show host, Peter Gzowski reminded me of that when I made a guest appearance on his show. To test my statement he asked me to research three questions: What was the unlisted home telephone number of businessman Conrad Black? What were the names of Canadian firms directly investing in South Africa which Statistics Canada refused to release? What were the names and addresses of the directors of an obscure corporation (the name of which was provided) which was based somewhere in the world, possibly in Canada?

I was given a week to complete the task and returned to face the unpredictable host. I had the answers, but it wasn't exciting to hear how the information was assembled. In fact, it seemed straightforward and simple: Black's phone number was obtained by a colleague of his; I assembled a list of Canadian firms directly investing in South Africa by making use of the research of two organizations (which were located by a simple literature search in the library), who routinely monitor such activity, and by using an inexpensive on-line computer search, "Inter-Corporate Ownership" database, to highlight Canadian firms with offices in South Africa; to track the obscure company I telephoned the federal Corporations Branch at the Department of Consumer and Corporate Affairs and was referred to the Ministry of Finance and Corporate

Relations for the province of British Columbia. This department, in turn, released the names of the directors and their home addresses.

Anybody could have answered those questions with a little know-how and practice. Obviously there wasn't anything mysterious in answering the questions. The key was in knowing where to go for what or in being able to figure out who to approach and how.

Of course, it isn't likely that you would ever want to intrude on someone's privacy by searching for an unlisted telephone number or to compile such corporate information. But most of us have serious information needs in our everyday personal and business lives that have a great deal of importance to us. Unfortunately, many of us rely on assumptions and guesswork to make decisions. Think back to the last time you purchased a faulty electrical appliance because you *assumed* it was a good buy—and later discovered that another, more reliable, product was available at considerably less cost. Or have you ever invested in the stock market without researching any companies —and lost money? Perhaps, during an interview with a prospective employer, you have been asked if you had any questions, and you've found yourself unable to utter a word because you weren't properly prepared—you assumed that *you* would be answering all the questions.

This book is intended to prevent those kinds of dilemmas. It is directed at anyone with serious, legitimate research needs. It is my belief that anyone can meet their information needs efficiently provided they have a *structure* on which to proceed. By structure I refer to three important ingredients: understanding the underlying *principles* of research, having a basic grasp of techniques, particularly *telephone techniques* for obtaining information, and having a sense of the *kinds* of information that exist.

This is not a traditional how-to book with hard and fast rules. Rather, it is an exploration of thought, focusing on the principles, techniques, and sources of this life skill we call research. In Chapters One through Eleven, information specialists are interviewed and in their own words describe how it is they are able to pull seemingly difficult-to-find information. By studying these interviews the researcher is introduced to telephone techniques and many different sources. But most importantly the researcher can see certain overlapping principles that all of the information specialists adhere to regardless of their different professions. These principles are very basic yet crucial to performing any kind of research. They are: acquiring an overview before commencing the actual research, formulating and refining questions, using secondary versus primary information, learning how to evaluate information, understanding the referral process, and recognizing research as a social skill.

It is worth elaborating on these principles here before reading the interviews in Part One and the reference sources listed in Part Two of the book.

ACQUIRING AN OVERVIEW

Before you begin to assemble information, ask yourself this question: "Am I ready to start my research?" Research is like reading: we bring meaning to the printed word, not the other way around. Having knowledge of a subject, we are able to understand what an author is trying to convey; otherwise, we could just open a textbook on advanced electronics and read. Most of us, however, need an *overview* of a topic in order to understand it. Without this overview, it is difficult to formulate specific research questions. Sometimes acquiring an overview can take longer than the actual research. You may have to read several books and interview many experts before coming to grips with a subject. But sometimes an appropriate book or article in an encyclopedia—even telephoning one expert—can suffice.

I was once asked to write an article for *Canadian Building* magazine on air rights in the construction industry. Because I didn't understand what air rights were, it was impossible to formulate specific questions in order to interview authorities on the subject. Magazine articles in my public library defined the concept this way: air rights are rights to lease or buy space above buildings, including transactions known as density transfers. I learned that air rights had been part and parcel of city planning for centuries. For example, the City of London leased air rights in 1209 to shopkeepers along London Bridge, permitting them to build and extend their shops upward. In the 1920s the Illinois Central Railroad leased the air rights on its property to developers to encourage development along an Illinois river.

Without this overview I could not have formulated intelligent, specific questions about what was initially a confusing concept.

FORMULATING AND REFINING QUESTIONS

Refining questions is an art in itself. Information specialists are very aware of this. If you were planning to do an online computer search and asked an information specialist, "Where can I find a list of articles on the effects of high technology on the economy that appeared in Canadian newspapers in 1983," your request would be turned down. A poorly-worded question like this wastes time and money and doesn't isolate useful information. The question could be reworded to "Where can I find a list of feature articles that appeared in the 'Report on Business' section of the *Globe and Mail* in January 1983 and that dealt with the effects of CAD/CAM high technology on Quebec's economy?"

This question is much more precise for a number of reasons: it lists the *kinds of articles* desired; a *specific publication* is requested; the *time frame* is exact; the *term* "high tech" is *defined* as CAD/CAM high technology; and the *geographical location* being examined is restricted to one province.

Refining questions is half the battle in any research. A friend once approached me with this question: "Do you know of any jobs?" He had asked the same question of friends and employment agencies, but was having no success. There were jobs available, but his problem was that he hadn't narrowed down his question so that he could search for them.

First I helped him formulate detailed questions. I asked him what his assets were. He had a graduate degree in education, had been a Y.M.C.A. director responsible for designing and teaching courses for five years, a director of a non-profit educational institution for eight years, and spoke fluent Italian. He had grown up in an Italian neighbourhood in Toronto and preferred to work with Italians in a non-profit organization. He found this type of setting more agreeable than a large corporate structure. The discussion clarified the main issues, so that the question now became: "How can I find employment as an instructor of adults in an Italian organization in Toronto?"

Next we were able to formulate other specific questions: "What Italian social service organizations exist in Toronto?" "Are there any associations that hire adult instructors?"

Once the questions were formulated, the investigation was relatively easy. A telephone call to City Hall enabled us to compile a list of all Italian social service agencies in Toronto. My friend determined which of these agencies provided educational programs, and he contacted them.

A quick look through the *Directory of Associations in Canada*, available in the public library, pinpointed the Ontario Society for Training and Development, an association that represents instructors of adults. It meets regularly and shares information on job openings.

As you might guess, my friend found the job he wanted. Such success is never guaranteed, of course, but proper research techniques enhance one's chances.

People setting out to research a subject often suffer "information paralysis"—an inability to define their information needs. I have encountered many people in a wide range of professions who have faced this problem. Here are a few of the most common types of questions before and after the students refined them:

"How can I find a person?" became "How can I locate Mrs. J.W. Jackson, who moved to Vancouver last year?"

"How much money did Brascan make in 1983?" became "What was the after-tax profit of Brascan's operations for the first quarter of 1983?"

"How do I start a trade union?" became "What legislation governs the formation of trade unions in British Columbia?"

"How can I find out if a bank will seize the car I am about to purchase because the present owner has used it as collateral for a loan he may have defaulted on?" became "Where can I get information on automobile liens in Ontario?"

"Where can I find out about housing prices?" became "Where can I find a list of housing prices for the city of Halifax?"

"Is there a cure for baldness?" became "Can male pattern baldness be cured?"

"Is there a link between diet and cancer?" became "Have any studies shown a correlation between breast cancer and diet in North America?"

SECONDARY VERSUS PRIMARY INFORMATION

The above questions—in fact, most questions—have already been answered. Somewhere, at some time, an expert has answered part or all of your question. This narrows your

research to *secondary* sources of information, and in nearly all
instances this information is available either in print or by telephoning the source. Your goal, then, is to locate indexes of published material and directories of experts and organizations.
Most public libraries keep these reference sources; both are
discussed in Chapter 12.

Locating experts isn't necessarily difficult. Newspaper and
magazine articles often quote experts, including thousands of
special interest groups in Canada who are obsessed with
various issues and spend incredible amounts of time researching their concerns. Tapping into them can turn into a goldmine.
Authors of books have specialized knowledge, so it's worth
walking into your local bookstore and asking the staff to look
up your subject heading in *Books In Print* (published by R. R.
Bowker). This way you can learn who is writing what and who
the publisher is. Through the publisher you can locate the
author in many instances. As well, don't overlook the footnotes
and bibliographies in books for leads. It can also pay off to call
your local university or community college and speak with the
public relations department to learn which experts exist in
various departments. Academic staff are often easily accessible. The ideas for tracking experts are endless. Let your
imagination take over, and you will find many other sources.

To return to the questions raised by my students, most of
these were answered by using indexes, directories, and government experts. The relative was located by calling Directory
Assistance in Vancouver. A telephone call to Brascan Ltd.
revealed the company's earnings. A librarian at the British
Columbia Ministry of Labour mailed a copy of the appropriate
provincial labour legislation. Information on automobile liens
in Ontario was obtained by a visit to the appropriate office of
the Ontario Ministry of Consumer and Commercial Relations
in Toronto. A cross-Canada survey of housing prices was
located in several newspaper articles. Several studies on baldness, as well as on breast cancer and diet correlations, surfaced in a directory of medical abstracts.

USING THE TELEPHONE

The telephone is a researcher's most valuable tool. I can think
of only a few instances where I could not obtain information
over the telephone. During my first few days as a copy boy at

the *Globe and Mail*, I witnessed a remarkable feat. The *Globe* kept a police-band radio in the newsroom to monitor potential sources, and late one night a bulletin thundered over it. A police shoot-out was taking place on Toronto's Madison Avenue. With seven minutes to the paper's editorial deadline, it was impossible to send a reporter to the scene, but everyone realized that heads would roll if the newspaper was scooped by another daily.

The city editor, Murray Burt, grabbed the typewriter and began pounding out the information as it came over the radio. After a few minutes he ran into the newspaper's library, searched through the city directory, and wrote down the telephone numbers of people living at addresses near the house where the shoot-out was happening. He then telephoned neighbours and asked for a description of events. He not only met the deadline but also produced a tightly-written story that appeared on the newspaper's front page the following morning.

EVALUATING SOURCES

In addition to limiting the amount of information you search for, you should learn to critically evaluate material by comparing your information with that provided by *different* sources. The more important the subject matter, the more sources you should have. Having only one source is not advisable for important research. Also, try to discover if a writer or interviewee has a bias. Slanted material is not neceessarily unusable—it may be used in context—but you must be aware of the bias in order to make good use of it.

USING REFERRALS

A researcher would like nothing better than to be able to tap one omniscient source. Alas, this is but a dream. Research, as you have probably discovered, often involves following up a series of referrals. You find a fact in one location, and this source leads you to another fact. And on it goes until a picture emerges.

The producer of CBC's "Marketplace" once hired me to interview homeowners who had found the controversial urea formaldehyde foam insulation in their homes. The idea originated via a letter received by a homeowner who was suing her real estate agent. She had been told when she purchased her house that it wasn't insulated with the foam, but in fact it was. The producer wanted me to look into similar cases.

I began by telephoning the lawyers involved in this case and asked for referrals. They knew of a few cases, and, by following up each of them, I was able to document thirty cases in a few days.

RESEARCH AS A SOCIAL SKILL

A good researcher needs to be able to interact with people. Research is unquestionably a social skill; people who get along with others find it easier to access information than those who are antagonistic. The best approach is to put people at ease. To achieve this, be relaxed, well-mannered, and conciliatory. An example comes to mind.

I once profiled Queen's Counsel Maxwell Bruce upon his appointment as head of Ontario's Residential Premises Rent Review Board. Bruce was then a director of Crown Trust, a Toronto firm offering real estate and mortgage loans. This meant that the new rent watchdog was a landlord with a potential conflict of interest.

Bruce appeared to be a nervous person, so I tried to put him at ease. I consciously raised topics for which he had a passion —he was very involved in environmental affairs, so we talked at great length about them. I didn't ask him directly about any conflict of interest, because this might have terminated the interview. Instead of taking an aggressive stance, I slipped in a seemingly innocent question, asking him whether he planned to drop any of his other activities. Bruce brought up the matter of Crown Trust himself and told me he had resigned his directorship to avoid a potential conflict of interest.

I could sense I had put him at his ease, and we parted on friendly terms. Later that evening he telephoned me at home to let me know that he still owned shares in Crown Trust and that he in fact had not yet resigned his directorship, but intended to shortly. I probably wouldn't have learned this any way other than by winning his trust.

Speaking of winning trust, you should remember that information should not be obtained in an illegal fashion. The sources presented in this book are public records, available to anyone. The techniques discussed are those used in many professions. There is no need to misrepresent yourself or lie to get information. If you do, you may be committing a criminal offence. After reading this manuscript, the late novelist Margaret Laurence telephoned me to say that she found the material "startling and alarming," in that so much information was available, particularly on people. But as a conveyor of ideas and truth, she also shared an optimism about the usages of this material and concluded that the ideas in this book were "deeply honourable."

In the following chapters you'll read about techniques used by specialists in different fields. You won't need to master every technique, but each one can be a valuable tool. For example, unless you work for a police force, you are unlikely to learn interrogation techniques, but police instructor Arthur R. Roberts's procedures for background preparation may be helpful in other situations. Use the edited interviews as a guide to doing your own research rather than as a rigid formula.

And remember, all information can be accessed!

APPROACHES

PART ONE

Telephone Interviewing Techniques

Paul McLaughlin is the author of Asking Questions: The Art of the Media Interview *(International Self-Counsel Press, 1986). Since 1973, he has worked as a writer, broadcaster, journalism instructor, and media trainer. He has won awards for his contributions to CBC Radio and national magazines such as* Toronto Life *and Financial Post's* Moneywise *magazine. He is currently Director of Media Services for The Multidimensional Group Inc. of Toronto. In this interview, he shows a clear understanding of many of the serious problems facing beginner interviewers as well as seasoned professionals. His solutions are directed at journalists but can certainly benefit anybody using the telephone.*

The telephone is a researcher's best friend. If you understand how to use it effectively, you can obtain information from an endless number of sources without having to leave your office or home. The greatest benefit, of course, is the amount of time you can save. Considering the value of that precious commodity, a researcher should strive to master telephone techniques with the same passion and determination that virtuoso performers put into refining their basic skills.

Before looking at specific telephone strategies, it is essential first of all to discuss the fear most people experience at the thought of telephoning someone they don't know and asking for help or information. This is a common and understandable problem. At the root of the fear are feelings that you might be rejected; that you don't have the right to impose on someone's time and knowledge; or that you'll make a fool of yourself.

These fears emerge from the conscious and unconscious mind in thoughts such as, "The person I have to call doesn't know me, has no reason to want to help me, and is going to be angry at me for wasting his time. He might confront me or even hang up. It's not going to be fun and I'm not looking forward to it. Besides, what right do I have to ask him to do my work for me? Why would a busy or important person, or anyone for that matter, agree to help a stranger? I have a lot of questions I need to ask and it's probably going to take too much of his time. Some of them are tough questions that he might not like to hear. Anyway, I'm afraid I'll embarrass myself by revealing how little I know about the subject. What if I ask a stupid question or don't understand one of his answers? If I expose my ignorance then he'll either ridicule me and/or end the conversation because I obviously don't know what I'm talking about." And so on, as a myriad of excuses plead their case to the psyche.

The effects of these fears vary, depending on the individual. For some, the effects are primarily feelings of apprehension or unpleasantness, especially prior to making the actual call. There may be some procrastination as a result, but the call eventually gets made. Once it does, the nervousness tends to go away. For projects involving a series of calls, often the biggest hurdle is making the first contact. After that a certain momentum develops and the process becomes easier.

But for others, the fears can have worse consequences. The prospect of phoning certain people might be so intimidating that the researcher simply doesn't try. "There's no way the person will speak to me," the thinking goes, "so why waste the time and effort." This type of avoidance is not uncommon. Even people who are usually confident can become unsettled at the thought of having to deal with certain individuals or situations they don't want to face. By predetermining the outcome, they convince themselves there's no point in calling.

In another scenario where the fears are more subtle, the call is made but the result is disastrous. The researcher is so rattled by his nervousness or feelings of devaluation that he's unable to communicate with confidence and clarity. Often the call ends up being brief and confused, reinforcing the researcher's belief that the call shouldn't have been made in the first place.

An equally unsuccessful outcome may occur when the researcher approaches the interviewee in either such a passive or pseudo-aggressive manner that the request is turned down. The passive researcher invites rejection by not being assertive enough. "I'm sorry to bother you when you're probably too busy to talk to me, and actually I'm not really sure you're the right person, but I was wondering if you might be able to help —but it's okay if you can't." This doormat style is often accompanied by an unclear presentation of the reason for the call. Inevitably, the combination of timidity and confusion results in an unsuccessful connection. Why would anyone, especially a busy person, respond otherwise?

The pseudo-aggressive version is just the flipside of the coin. In this case the researcher overcompensates for his anxiety by being obnoxious and bullying, substituting feelings of his own intimidation by trying to intimidate the other person. This approach also sets up rejection. The interviewee is either turned off by the rudeness or scared by the prospect of speaking to such an unpleasant stranger. Even if the bullying coerces the interviewee into conversation, the odds are against the exchange achieving its potential, as the interviewee is likely to be guarded in his responses.

There is no magical antidote to eliminate these fears. They exist, to one degree or another, in everyone. However, it is possible to lessen their negative impact, so that the fears are at least under control and often diminished.

The most effective way to lessen their impact is to acknowledge them. That simple, but often difficult, step makes it possible for the problem to be dealt with consciously. When you understand the reason for your anxiety, some of its magnitude is lost. By identifying the cause of your apprehension, you can develop a strategy to overcome it. To help make the acknowledgement and the creation of strategies easier, there are several factors to keep in mind:

- You're not the only one with these fears (a point worth repeating). Most veteran researchers and journalists experience them throughout their career.

- There is a form of salesmanship involved in the process. While many people are not comfortable with "selling themselves," it is necessary to acquire a degree of salesmanship in order to convince people to co-operate with you. Now, this doesn't mean becoming disingenuous or dishonest. It does mean, however, that you think about what needs to be transmitted to the prospective interviewees in order to make them calm and want to help you. In other words, you have to develop a personal style.

- That style should be as natural as possible. You don't have to sound like a K-Tel announcer or any of the other archetypical salespersons. In fact, if you attempt to put on a voice or style that is contrary to your nature, in most cases it will turn people off. Obviously, if you have wit and charm, they are to your advantage. But if you are inclined to shyness, that doesn't mean you can't be impressive. If you are clear, prepared, and genuine, you can make a powerful impact no matter whether you're extroverted or introverted. Many shy people prefer the telephone to meeting in person. It makes them feel more at ease because many of the dynamics of personal encounters, such as appearances and surroundings, are eliminated.

- Be aware of what it's like to be on the receiving end of your telephone call. Just as you may be nervous in calling, so may the recipient be anxious as well. If you're both freaking out, and neither of you understands the reason, you can increase each other's anxieties. Being questioned is unnerving for most people. Remember your own feelings at being questioned by a customs official, police officer, boss, teacher, or in some cases, a parent. Most of those memories, especially the ones from childhood, have strong assocations of guilt or anxiety. A journalist, or anyone gathering information, can trigger off those ingrained responses. Of equal consideration are the consequences the person faces in speaking with you. In this day and age, there is justifiable caution when giving out information to a journalist or anyone else. Many organizations have a policy about who can say what to the media and/or public. Although some people hide behind that unnecessarily and refuse to divulge information that they should release, you must be sensitive to the reasons those restrictions may exist. No matter how loud you yell, if the person faces the possible loss of his job by speaking to you, you won't and shouldn't want to convince him to talk except in such special cases as when public safety is involved. Even then, you're more likely to achieve your goals by collaborating with the person, through the establishment of an agreement under which his or her identity is protected. The more attuned you are to the other person's circumstances, the better able you will be to alleviate *his* fears. By doing so, you increase greatly the chance of gaining that person's trust and co-operation.

- If the person declines to speak with you, it is important not to take the rejection personally. You cannot force someone who doesn't want to speak to you to do so. At the same time, it's essential for your own development to assess whether the refusal was a result of your actions. If you decide it was—that, for example, in your pitch for help you forgot to mention a significant piece of information— perhaps you could call back and try again. At the least, you should learn for the next time. If you know you were thorough, you have to let go of feelings of failure or rejection. It's the nature of the work that it doesn't allow you to compel people to do your bidding. If you've gone the distance on your end, what more can you do?

If you can overcome your fears, you'll discover that when approached intelligently and with sensitivity, most people will respond. Sensitivity, by the way, shouldn't be confused with wimpishness. If you sense that a person needs to feel the urgency of your request, then you may have to be quite aggressive to get your point across. At another time, you may need to be very quiet, very understated to make the person feel relaxed. In other words, through intelligence and creativity, you devise a conscious strategy that is genuinely sensitive to the needs of those involved in the communication. If you prefer to try and bulldoze them, that may work in some instances—but it will not bring victory in the long term.

More significant than the question of whether it works is that you won't feel good about yourself. Unless the idea of behaving like an unpleasant bill collector appeals to you, there is a great deal of value in refining a personal phone style that is assertive but not obnoxious. To develop such a style, four basic points should be considered: preparation, politeness, persistence, and creativity.

Preparation   Planning is essential and will contribute greatly to the reduction of anxiety. The more you're prepared, the more you'll be relaxed. When you're relaxed, you'll be more confident and intuitive.

There are two aspects of preparation to consider. One is the purely empirical. It involves taking the time to plan the purpose of the interview. Too many people pick up the telephone and start making research calls without really knowing what they want to ask. It is a horrible sensation to go blank a few minutes into the conversation. Apart from the humiliation, you will probably have blown the opportunity to use the person as a source. It's hard to be humble enough to call back and ask for a second chance because you weren't prepared enough (even though you may have to do just that).

The guidelines for preparation are very simple:

- Before calling, ask yourself the purpose of the call. It may be beneficial to write down the main reason or focus of the interview.

- Make notes on what points you want to cover. This can mean preparing a list of questions. It's important, however, not to read from a list. Engage the interviewee in conversation and use the written material as a back-up to make sure you haven't forgotten something. Of all the questions, the most important is the first. That sets the tone for the interview and can get the ball rolling. From there you can follow up with a natural progression of responses. If you flail about without a clear first question, it can shake your confidence and signal you are not prepared. Remember that during your first phone call, the person you speak to may ask what questions you want answered. Don't presume that because you're calling to arrange an interview you don't need to be ready with your questions. Also be prepared for the interviewee to say, "Okay, let's do it now." If you had an agenda planned with next week in mind, you could be put into a most embarrassing position if you're not ready to go.

- Determine whether the person you're calling can answer the questions. He or she may be the wrong source. If you believe that may be the case, be prepared for the phone call to be simply a stepping stone to the correct contact. It is not unusual in research to have to make several calls before you end up with the best person. In each case, you should elicit all the assistance you can from each person, using questions such as, "Do you know the name of someone who can answer my questions? Do you have that person's phone number? Do you think he'll be receptive to my call? Any advice on how to speak to him? Can I mention that I was speaking to you?" This last point is very valuable. When you approach the next person, you have what amounts to a personal reference, tenuous as it may be. People like to know how you came to call them. If you can mention someone they know, it makes them more relaxed. If it's someone you both know, it's even more beneficial.

- There will be times when you need to do research before you make the call. It generally depends on how important the interview is. Decide whether you need to do research on the subject and/or person before you make the call. Many researchers get lazy and figure the person they're contacting should supply all the information. But many interviewees—especially the ones who are frequently contacted by the media—become irritated at doing the interviewer's homework. The ground rule is to do as much as possible beforehand, within the time and budget restraints. There is also an element of respect involved. If you phone a corporate president and know nothing about him or his company—information that could easily have been gathered—you may irritate him to the point that he won't want to co-operate. Conversely, you can transform a reluctant guest into a willing collaborator by discreetly flattering him or her with your knowledge of their accomplishments.

- Make sure you know how you're going to introduce yourself and explain the purpose of your call. Whether the first person you speak to is a secretary or the intended interviewee, you must feel confident about the wording and then present it in a clear fashion. How you do this will make a most important impression on whoever you're calling. If you are unclear and clumsy in your use of language, you risk having the person dismiss you as being unprofessional. For example, here is a poor introduction: "Hello, this is Paul. Is Stephen Overbury possibly able to speak with me?" This kind of introduction has many faults. It flounders; it uses *negative* phrases such as "possibly able," which often lead to rejection. Also, this approach invites many questions such as, "Who exactly are you?" "Where are you from?" A more positive approach is "Hello, this is Paul McLaughlin of The Multidimensional Group Inc. I'm calling for Stephen Overbury to confirm an appointment to discuss the promotion of his book." This is a more *positive* way of introducing yourself. I have provided credentials by using a full personal name and company name.

The other aspect of preparation deals with anticipating the emotional context of the communication. Some of the factors have been mentioned earlier, such as being aware of your own emotional state and that of the other person. Coming to terms with emotional states is just as important—if not more so—than writing down questions and working on your opening pitch.

There are several points to consider that will help you with this type of preparation:

- Put yourself in the place of the person you'll be calling. Try to imagine who he is: Is he in a position of power? What authority does he have to speak publicly or release information? What are his needs in relation to you? If you know his age or any other personal information, consider whether it will play a part in your communication. If you are young and the person is considerably older, be prepared for that to have an effect on the interview. The older person may not take you seriously; you may have to win the person's respect, which can be done through your knowledge and professionalism. It also helps to demonstrate your respect for someone older and more experienced than yourself. The more you prepare a mental profile of the person, the easier it will be to create a positive strategy to approach him.

- Then do an emotional check on yourself. Is there anything about this interview that is disturbing you? Is it the subject matter? The specific individual involved? The type of individual? Realize that if you are rattled, one of the ways of calming down is to know that you're thoroughly prepared. Another is to visualize the interview taking place, going through in your mind the many ways it could evolve. Don't run away from any potential pitfalls. Instead, allow yourself to see them happen and include in your imagining process the same problems being overcome.

- Consider what tone you will use for certain questions, especially those you anticipate might be sensitive or inflammatory. It's important to be aware of your tone throughout the communication but even more so for areas that might cause the interview to break down. People often find it difficult to ask unpleasant questions without being either too apologetic or too cold. In both cases, it's because they don't feel comfortable with the intensity of the subject. While the strategies required to find the right tone are too complex to discuss here in detail, a couple of points might help. One is that if you're going to ask a question, don't apologize for doing so. In respect to your tone, err on the side of sensitivity rather than brusqueness. Don't moralize or judge the person in the wording of your question. Give people the opportunity to explain their position. Don't be afraid to ask a tough question, as long as it's fair, or if it's a point that has been made public. It's unlikely the interviewee will be shocked by the question. It's how you ask that's more telling than what you ask.

- Equally important, of course, are the order of your questions and their *wording*. Although it can pay to ask a direct, hard-hitting question up front, there are also situations where you are advised to bury key questions well into the interview—and to word them in non-threatening ways.

- As a final guideline, bear in mind that there has to be something in it for the person you contact. Too many journalists, for example, expect people to help them without thinking or caring about the person on the other end of the phone. That means you have to take the time to explain exactly what you're doing. You may have to flatter them, call upon the public's right to have the information, offer them the chance to be quoted or acknowledged for their contribution, or give them a chance to set the record straight or to get back at someone who has wronged them. If they feel that you're not just in it for yourself, they'll be far more likely to co-operate.

Politeness   As discussed earlier, politeness will not only contribute to your peace of mind but will also result in far more victories than will some kind of verbal extortion. That conclusion is inevitable if you put yourself in the other person's shoes. How would you feel about a stranger who calls you up and in a rude and demanding tone, threatens you if you fail to do his bidding immediately, hangs the possibility of being referred to negatively in the media over your head, accuses you of trying to cover up some injustice, or is in some other way unpleasant and pushy?

Compare that to someone who is considerate, calm, straightforward, and generally reasonable to deal with. If you are a secretary and you have to chose between passing on a message from the former or the latter, which message would you give your blessing to?

Politeness, however, should not be confused with weakness. If the person you're communicating with is not co-operating, that has to be confronted. But there's a difference between starting an argument, which is always a waste of energy, and becoming more aggressive in your tone. The key point is whether you have a righteous cause for being upset. For example, you have politely called a press officer for several days to get an interview with a politician and have been promised that it will be arranged. You are then told it has been cancelled and won't be rescheduled. That is cause for becoming upset and confronting the press officer. Saying no from the outset is his and the politician's prerogative. But leading you on, if that's what you think has happened, is not acceptable and an angry response is warranted. In some cases, the intensity of your anger may result in the decision being reconsidered. However, if you're told from the outset that no interview will be granted and you throw a verbal tantrum, that's not acceptable.

Persistence   There is a strong case, though, for *persistence*. You shouldn't take no for an answer until you're convinced that there's absolutely no chance of winning. There are many stories of interviews finally being granted because someone called a secretary for days or weeks just to check up politely on the potential interviewee's itinerary. Over time, a relationship developed between the caller and the secretary. Eventually, the secretary became an ally and convinced the boss to make an exception and agree to the interview. Nor does the scenario have to include an intermediary. The calls may be made, at reasonable intervals, directly to the intended guest. A letter may also be sent directly to the boss with a copy to the secretary to supplement the calls.

A variation on this scenario can take place in a shorter time span, such as during a day when a deadline is looming. If you have to reach a politician for an interview, you may end up calling his office many times that day. If that happens, it's essential to enlist the collaboration of the secretary or liaison person. Apart from politeness and humour, you should always try to create a reason for calling back. For example, ask for a time by which you can expect an answer. If there's no call forthcoming by that time, it gives you permission to call back. Then set another deadline. Explore other avenues of contact with the person you wish to speak with. Ask what his schedule is that day. Where is he now? If he's in a meeting, could a message be taken in or given to him at break or lunch? If he's at a restaurant, which one? Does he have a beeper? Never give up until you've run out of time or ideas.

Although most situations are straightforward, your creativity may be called into play any time when it comes to finding people, getting past the palace guard, or talking someone into giving you an interview. There are no rules for creativity that can be laid out as a blueprint. Most examples of creative genius were inspired in the moment. However, it's necessary to distinguish between artistic manoeuvres and unethical deceptions.

Let us say you're having trouble getting through to a company president named Jack Hamilton. You feel his secretary is not passing on your messages. So, instead of calling in your usual way, which means identifying yourself and your purpose, the next time you ask to speak to "Jack" in a demanding tone. When the secretary asks who's calling, you reply "Helen," giving only your first name. This time your tone is impatient and imperious. If the secretary puts your call through, which is quite possible, the deception is minor. It would then be wise to explain to Hamilton what you did and assure him that his secretary was not an accomplice. He then may agree to speak with you, either out of admiration for your pluck or in resignation to the fact you're on the phone with him anyway.

However, the distance between that kind of harmless misrepresentation and a form of entrapment is not that far. Let us say you're doing a story on the safety standards at a local tanning salon. The owners refuse to grant you an interview. However, you call the salon and speak to the receptionist while posing as a potential customer. Through leading questions, you get the receptionist to say that it doesn't matter how long you stay under ultraviolet lights. She also says other things that imply that the salon has no interest in maintaining safe standards. The next day you write a story in the newspaper quoting an unnamed receptionist at the firm (how many would they have?) in a context that will likely result in her firing.

What she said may have been accurate, although she may just have been overzealous in her desire to sell a membership. However, she should not have been put into a position of making remarks that would be quoted without knowing what was at stake. Here the end does not justify the means. The entrapment was not fair or even necessary because the information could have been obtained by the journalist's signing up for a membership and finding out for himself what the standards were.

Without going into the many ethical intricacies of these types of situations, suffice it to say that you should err most strongly on the side of fairness and truthfulness. A good measuring stick is to ask how you would feel if the deception were practised on you.

Creativity   An example of the triumph of creativity and persistence is told by Bob McKeown, now the co-host of "the fifth estate," about an exclusive interview a researcher lined up when McKeown was host of the Montreal CBC Radio program "Daybreak" in 1979. It was the day following the takeover of the American Embassy in Teheran.

"The day after the takeover, our researcher, Avi Coehn, suggested we try to get an interview with the Ayatollah," McKeown remembers. "This was 6 a.m. in Montreal and we said, 'Sure, Avi,' and thought no more of it.

"Just before 9 a.m. and the end of the program, the red light on the studio phone started flashing and I asked Avi, who was in the control room, who was on the line.

'Guess,' he said, with a triumphant look on his face.

'The Ayatollah?'

'No, but it's someone who speaks English and is sitting beside the Ayatollah.'

"What he had done was to phone Teheran over and over again all morning. You have to go through Paris, which he did twelve times, until he got an operator in Teheran who spoke French. He asked for the Ayatollah's number, but it was unlisted. He then called back another twelve times until he got another French-speaking operator and told her he'd just been doing an interview with the Ayatollah for CBC and had been cut off. If she knew what was good for her and didn't want to invoke the wrath of the leader of the Islamic revolution, she'd better put him back through. This intimidated her enough that she gave him a number to call.

"The number was for a phone on the desk in an area where, under Islamic law, the Ayatollah would meet at a certain time each week to deal with problems and representations from mayors of the various Islamic states. After seven calls to that number, Avi reached a mayor who spoke French and English.

" 'Would you know what the Ayatollah feels about what's taken place at the embassy?' Avi asked. 'Why don't I ask him?' the mayor replied, 'He's right here.'

"A few minutes later, with the mayor acting as an interpreter, we had the first interview with the Ayatollah after the hostages were taken."

The qualities Cohen displayed—persistence, ingenuity, moxie, and a basic understanding of human nature—are characteristics worth acquiring and refining if you want to learn the art of persuading people to talk to you on the telephone.

A Journalist's Notebook

At only twenty-seven years of age, reporter John Zaritsky won the first of many prestigious awards, the Ford Foundation Fellowship, to attend the Washington Journalism Center. There he was offered a job by the Washington Post *as a cub reporter. Concerned that he would be spending his best years working on insignificant stories, Zaritsky turned down the offer, and the paper hired its second choice—Carl Bernstein.*

Two years later, as an investigative and political reporter for the Globe and Mail, *Zaritsky won a National Newspaper Award for a series of articles which revealed that Ontario cabinet minister Darcy McKeough had approved the subdivision of land in which he had had a financial interest. Largely as a result of the articles, Ontario's conflict-of-interest legislation was tightened up.*

Since 1975, Zaritsky has worked for the CBC as producer of its highly acclaimed investigative series, "the fifth estate." Zaritsky's credits with that program include some of its more contentious and controversial reports and an Oscar-winning documentary, "Just Another Missing Kid," an investigation into the death of nineteen-year-old Eric Wilson and the inefficiencies of the American judicial system.

His other accomplishments include a PBS "Frontline" show on domestic violence and winning the coveted "Award For Excellence" (A.C.E.) for co-producing (with his wife, Virginia Storring) "Rapists: Can They Be Stopped?"

Zaritsky explains that there is no mystery to research. For him it boils down to hard work and persistence. For him there are no hard and fast rules; rather, each story dictates a new approach to gathering information.

In this edited interview, he gives examples of when to use a "soft" or "hard" approach in interviews. He reveals how to win the trust of sources. In describing the McKeough affair, he demonstrates how to invent strategies that open the doors to information and where to go if these doors close.

Zaritsky also explains how he used basic sources for some of his biggest stories, including interviews with municipal planners, land registry files, and company records available through the government. He cautions researchers against relying on only one source and provides a list of questions to ask when dealing with any source. Body language, and the techniques he used to con a con into releasing RCMP documents, are also explored.

There is a philosophy that I adopt in all my work: I don't want *any* surprises. I want to learn everything there is to know about a particular subject—and from every conceivable angle. If I am working on an investigative story, I always try to put myself in the position of the person I'm interviewing; I try to anticipate what their defence may be. Otherwise, I may end up with a surprise that can devastate my story. In my work I have to be very complete.

Perhaps the biggest research challenge of my career came when I was at the *Globe and Mail*. I got a tip from a stranger who would not identify himself and was quite nervous and agitated on the telephone. He told me that when Darcy McKeough had been Ontario Minister of Municipal Affairs, he had approved the subdivision of some land that he owned or had a financial interest in. On the surface, it was a great story. It meant that McKeough had a direct conflict of interest because he had used his public position for private gain. But what the source didn't know, or was unwilling to say, was where the land was; nor would he say where he had acquired this information.

I began the research in the most logical spot—in Chatham, McKeough's home. I went there to acquaint myself with the town and find out about the subdivisions that had been built around it.

I went to the town hall and created some every innocuous reason for my interest. You can get a lot of information out of people as long as you seemingly don't have any bad reason to want it. I said the *Globe* was doing a story on towns and cities and on the growth problems they were experiencing. I spent a week or two learning what the town limits were, what growth the town had experienced, and talking to a lot of town planners to determine the kind of subdivision of land that had occurred in the area.

It was a very difficult situation. This was Kent County, and the McKeough family was wealthy and established. Darcy McKeough was a local hero and was known in the county as the "Duke of Kent." The least sign that I was trying to expose a highly prominent man—the local Member of Parliament and the second most powerful man in the Ontario government— and the doors would have closed immediately.

During these initial weeks of research, most of my information came from interviews. There was no way I could do the title searches without getting a lot of people nervous about what I was doing. After a few weeks I still didn't have proof of what I had been told over the phone; I didn't know whether there was even a grain of truth to it. But by then I was familiar enough with Chatham to start my research in the local land registry office. I started searching the titles for a lot of the newer subdivisions. I didn't know what McKeough owned; I just kept searching and eventually found a number of companies that had sold land for subdivisions in the Chatham area. Then I simply copied the names of those companies, went to the Companies Services Branch of the Ministry of Consumer and Commercial Relations in Toronto, and researched their boards of directors. Lo and behold, McKeough's name appeared on one of the boards, and then his brother's name appeared.

Then the delicate task began—determining whether the minister himself had signed the documents approving the subdivision, or whether they had been signed in his name by a bureaucrat. To answer this question I started, in a general, unintimidating way, to learn how subdivision controls worked. I wasn't after specifics at this stage, just general information on the process. I drew up a list of questions: How was a subdivision approved? What was the involvement of the ministry? What did the minister do? What was his power? Did he ever reject an application?

I established that the minister had real power and wasn't a rubber stamp figure. Then, having established the general process, I moved on to the case in question. Once I knew how it was done for all subdivisions, I could finally ask: in this specific instance, was this process carried out?

The final answer was yes, it had. The minister had actually signed the documents. The series of articles on this subject led to McKeough's resignation.

Another important guideline I follow when researching a topic is: try to avoid trusting one source. Always examine the motivation of people. Ask yourself: Why are they telling me this? What's in it for them? Who are they? What axe do they have to grind? Always be aware of the fact that people give you information for a reason, so check and recheck and confirm from other sources. A one-source story is a very dangerous story. But also keep in mind that though people have an axe to grind, don't let it stop you from using their information. Sometimes the information can be accurate—and most important— verifiable.

Here is a case in point. I once worked on a story that involved a man who had broken into an RCMP detachment in Eastern Ontario. He had rifled the safe and stolen confidential documents. I was working for the *Globe and Mail* at the Ontario provincial gallery at the time, pursuing a number of investigative stories. I received a call from Morton Shulman, then a Member of Parliament. He had been contacted by this man, who was trying to sell him the stolen documents, which he said included evidence that the Mounties had been using juveniles as paid informers without their parents' knowledge or consent. Shulman said he couldn't touch the story, but he could put the man in contact with me.

The *Globe* and I then faced a real problem; if we bought the documents, we could be charged with receiving stolen property. We certainly didn't want to pay for the information, but at the same time we wanted as much of it as we could acquire, because it sounded as if the public had a legitimate right to know about it.

I held a series of hair-raising meetings around the Ontario legislature with the man, but at some point the Ontario Provincial Police became aware of them. So the meetings had to become even more clandestine. I kept leading the man on, saying we weren't really sure he had anything that was worthwhile and that he would have to give us proof that he had what he said he had.

Finally he fell for it and produced a list of the RCMP informers and the amounts they were paid, their names, their ages, and everything else to prove that he had all this other material. The "other material" included documents on what to do in case of a nuclear attack, none of which I was keen to acquire. What I really wanted was what he gave me. We got our story.

My involvement with "the fifth estate" documentary, "Just Another Missing Kid," began when we were approached by the parents of the murdered youth, Eric Wilson. They knew part of the story, but only part. They explained their experiences with different police forces, their own search for Eric through Nebraska and Colorado, the lack of co-operation and the indifference of the authorities they had met. One of the things they couldn't understand was why the killer of their son had been arrested in Eric's van and subsequently released.

So our research addressed several questions: What were the circumstances of the arrest? What charges had been laid against the killer? When had he been released? Why had he been released?

The circumstances of each story dictate the approach and philosophy you use to gather information. In this case we went to the American police and judicial authorities, including the Assistant District Attorney who had been in charge of the case. And, rather than adopting a tough, hard-nosed, adversarial stance, we approached them as Canadians who were unfamiliar with the American judicial system and, like the family, simply didn't understand how these rather strange and seemingly inexplicable events had occurred. We asked them to please help us, as foreigners, understand the situation. Brian Vallee, the associate producer working with me, and I talked to these officials briefly over the telephone at first, in a neutral fashion, then visited them and spoke with them extensively for several days. We told them that we wanted to understand the American judicial system as it worked in this particular case. This approach put them more at ease, especially because they were themselves quiet critics of the system. We wouldn't have won their support had we used a "Sixty Minutes," guns-drawn approach, demanding, "Why, Mister D.A., did you let this hoodlum go when you clearly had him?"

A lot of researchers approach their work with preconceived notions about what has actually happened, who the good guys and the bad guys are. Their know-it-all attitude is quickly picked up by their potential sources, who often sense this hostility and built-in bias. Instead, the researcher's or investigative reporter's primary purpose should be to encourage the subject to talk. This is a cardinal principle. Anything that accomplishes the goal of people relaxing and talking to you yields better results than if you do a lot of the talking to show you know what it's all about. In a sense it boils down to submerging your ego. Sometimes you have to play dumb.

The biggest difference in my approach to research now, as opposed to when I began eighteen years ago, is that I'm a lot softer. I play dumb more often, I'm far more neutral, and I concentrate more on listening than on asking questions. I approach people in a more open-ended way, and I am really willing to listen to everyone's side of the story; as a result, I think I get harder stories now.

Your approach also depends on the constraints of time and money. First, establish some sort of communication with the subject. Bear in mind that a lot of people are busy. You can't, for instance, interview a cabinet minister and fish around for neutral subjects to discuss. However, approaching a topic slowly is often the best policy, even by talking about something as mundane as the weather or the town you live in.

The best kind of interview is arranged on a person's home ground—at their house, as opposed to their office. Restaurants and bars aren't a great idea, because they are public places; some people are nervous about talking in public. Your object should be to win people's trust and confidence. You achieve this by proving you are a sympathetic and understanding individual who isn't going to expose them and that you are doing something worthwhile, something they can believe in.

I obtained police and court files through my contacts on the "Missing Kid" story by adhering to these principles. These records were, of course, invaluable, because my task was to find out everything about the lives of the two killers, from the time they were born until the time they committed the murder.

I also had to interview a lot of different people, some of whom were not always honest, so I used their body language to tip me off when they were about to lie. I can tell when people are fudging, because I look a lot at their eyes. Eye contact tells me a lot: very few people who are about to lie look you right in the face—there is always some slight movement around the eyes that breaks eye contact. This goes back to our childhood. We rarely ever looked into our parents' faces and lied. It's ingrained. One man I interviewed for "Missing Kid," for example, lied and lied and lied. And at times he also told the truth. But when he lied, there was a nervous twitch on one side of his face; it was almost imperceptible, but it was reliable.

Here's another important rule for me in any story I'm working on: never betray a source. It pays to stick to this rule. In the early 1970s, I wrote a series of articles for the *Globe and Mail* about the Ontario government's purchase of land from a company with several prominent Tories on its board of directors. The directors had bought the land cheaply and sold it shortly after to the government for a healthy profit. The articles led to an official inquiry in which I was a star witness. The entire focus of the inquiry became how I had acquired my information. The judge ordered me to divulge the names of my sources. I refused. He threatened to throw me in jail. I still refused. He finally decided not to make a martyr out of me and instead fined me $500. It was a great boon for me, because it established, publicly, that I would not betray a source. Thanks to the Ontario government, I was given impeccable advertising to enable me to carry on my work. From that point on, nervous civil servants remembered that I had stood the test.

As I mentioned earlier, the circumstances of each story dictate my approach. Sometimes it's extremely difficult to even confront the key person. Let me give you an example.

I worked on another series of articles for the *Globe* about certain firms which were receiving an inordinate amount of business from the Ontario government without submitting tenders. One company was owned by an individual who was well shielded from reporters by his secretaries. I could never get through this protective office shield. To talk to him, I first found out where he lived. I knew his name and used the Might Directories at the library to find his home address. I knew from chasing him around his office that he left work around five and that, given the length of the drive from his office to his home, he would arrive home at about five-thirty. So I made sure that I was at his home at five-fifteen. He clearly knew I wanted to speak with him, and he had been avoiding me. When he arrived, I simply got out of my car, gave him my name, said that I had been attempting to reach him for a number of days, and here I was. He didn't have anything to say to me, but he did say, "No comment." That was crucial information at that stage; until then my only information had been that he was unavailable for comment. This new information, one sentence in a story, revealed that he had had a chance to offer some explanation.

There are no hard and fast rules in research. Although I've pointed out that playing dumb in interviews can work, I must admit that I have had to be very hard-nosed on a number of occasions. I've interviewed people using a very tough approach and pretended that I knew a lot more than I actually did, in the hope that they would present their side of the story. I've worked with other reporters and used a classic police technique, "good cop, bad cop," in which one reporter plays at being on the interviewee's side and the other is hostile. You create conflict with the other reporter and try to force a confession out of the person you are interviewing. This technique has worked, too.

I took this approach with one of the best investigative reporters in the country, Gerald McAuliffe, on stories for the *Globe*. We were after Ontario civil servants who were trying to hide shady land deals, including purchases of land along the Niagara Escarpment. In one interview McAuliffe played the tough guy and became verbally violent and accusatory. I asked him to leave the room. Then, in the privacy of the civil servant's office, I explained that McAuliffe was a hot-headed individual who sometimes got carried away. It was difficult to put the brakes on him, so to protect himself, the government official should give me his side of the story. I told him I sympathized with him for being browbeaten and unfairly accused. I also said that if he would explain his side, I would do everything I could to make sure McAuliffe understood that there was indeed another point of view. The official then began to reveal a story far more implicating, and reaching a higher level of government, than we had imagined possible.

I have also found it advantageous to work on stories with another researcher. Each person operates as a brake on the other, so you don't get carried away. You have someone to help you recheck your facts and ensure that the story is accurate.

I have mentioned that you can get a lot of information out of people as long as you don't seem to have any bad reason for wanting it. I used this approach when I wrote the land story (referred to on page 21), which led to the Ontario government inquiry. The articles, roughly told, stated that the Ontario government had purchased 506 acres of land for a park at the forks of the Credit River, northwest of Toronto, from a corporation called Caledon Mountain Estates Limited. I found out that the company's board of directors included several prominent Tories. These board members had purchased the land for $805 an acre and resold it to the government within two years for $1,450 an acre. Had these Tories been tipped off through their political connections that the land was going to be used to create a park? Had they taken advantage of inside information?

I started my research by searching the land titles of the properties involved; they told me the original purchase price and the history of each piece of land in question. Then I had to establish that certain board members were highly-placed Tories. This was tricky, but I concocted a quite innocent reason for wanting a list of all the delegates who had attended the 1971 leadership convention that had resulted in the election of William Davis. The Conservative party gave me the list of all the delegates. I compared the names on this list with those of the land purchasers and found some of them to be the same.

After the first stories started to appear, one ministry began to refuse to give out information. There was a high degree of paranoia, and I soon realized that I wasn't going to get any information out of that ministry. So here's another principle in research: if you can't get the information from one source, try another. A lot of the same information is kept in several government departments, so you have to find the department that will give it to you.

In this instance, that's precisely what I did. First of all, I tried to understand how government, and in this case how the Ontario government, went about purchasing land. I found there was another department that handled the actual mechanics of land purchasing. With the heat on one specific department, and understanding how land purchasing occurs, I approached the other department. Again I used a seemingly innocuous reason for my inquiries. I located a middle-level civil servant who gave me the information that was absolutely confidential elsewhere: what the government had paid for the land. Until then that hadn't been made public.

When I joined CBC's "fifth estate," I used a lot of the same basic techniques I had employed as a print journalist. For instance, I once worked on a documentary on the Canadian International Development Agency (CIDA). I didn't want to produce a traditional documentary on foreign aid, discussing the terrible needs and poverty of the Third World, nor did I want to do another show on the screw-ups of CIDA. I saw much more fundamental problems with the Canadian foreign aid effort. In the end I found that under the guise of helping the needy, Canada was basically helping inefficient, non-competitive industries at home. It was allowing them to foist inappropriate technology, products, and services on the Third World—all in the name of charity and foreign aid. This really wasn't appropriate, nor was it helping the people whom Canadian citizens wanted to help.

That was an exhausting, six-month research effort conducted by Mary Frances Morrison and me. We started the research by reading every piece of literature we could find on foreign aid. This gave us a rudimentary grasp of the subject, the facts.

Then we talked to as many experts in Canada as we could find. Some of these contacts emerged from the literature search; others were obtained by contacting universities. We had to find people locally, because our funds didn't permit us to travel outside Canada to do research. We had to know the situation before we left Canada to film the story. And the only way we could find out what had happened in countries thousands of miles away was to talk to people who had been there.

The Third World countries were not anxious to be critical of foreign aid programs—in a sense, to bite the hand that was feeding them. We were not allowed into Botswana, where there was a project we were particularly interested in and one we thought was a good case study for bad foreign aid. To get into the country, we disguised ourselves as tourists, carrying Kodak cameras. Then we travelled to the "Sudbury of Botswana," an area where there was nothing but an awful iron smelter. We aroused the suspicions of the local secret police and had all sorts of wild adventures as a result.

The object of our visit to Botswana was to film the CIDA project. To do this we had to sneak a film crew into the country from South Africa. The crew had convinced the Botswana authorities that they were doing a wildlife film for the South African Broadcasting Corporation. It worked. We met the crew at the smelter, got our footage, and were able to show what CIDA money had built, as well as the squalid conditions the workers lived in.

I must caution prospective researchers about the stories I've described. It is true that there are stories, such as the one about the stolen Mountie records on pages 18 and 19, for which you can obtain the information you need if you can talk to the right person and if you handle your source properly. But a lot of stories are not like that; a lot of stories do not involve one magical fount of knowledge that you can tap and then come away with an entire story. Many stories are like working on pieces of a jigsaw puzzle. You fit one piece in one place, and it enables you to fit in another piece somewhere else. Two pieces enable you to fit in the third piece, and so on.

Getting Tough:
Police Interrogation

Meet Arthur R. Roberts, a leading police instructor and an expert on forcing criminals to talk. He spent thirty-five years with the Calgary Police Department and retired as the commanding officer of its Detective Unit. He still lectures on interviewing and interrogating techniques to police forces across Canada.

Most of us can avoid an interrogation to get information. Nevertheless, the preparation that Roberts recommends and the other observations he makes in this edited interview, reveal principles that can be applied in everyday interview situations.

Interviewing is an art that can be learned, but it is not a science. It cannot be rigidly guided by a fixed set of rules or principles. It is your personality, combined with the skills you have acquired, that lead to success. The only way to become an efficient interviewer or interrogator is to gain experience through practice. Remember the words of Sigmund Freud: "Man loves to talk. He cannot keep a secret." Truth oozes out of every pore.

I believe this. People can't keep a secret—all you have to do is make it easy for them to talk. Eighty percent of all people will confess to a crime; the trick is to make yourself easy to talk to. Give them an ear to listen and a shoulder to cry on. Ask the right question in the right manner at the right time, and they will give you the right answer.

There are two basic techniques for obtaining information: interviewing and interrogating. An interrogation is an interview with stress. In an interview we ask questions without creating stress; in an interrogation we ask questions that create psychological stress.

Whether you interview or interrogate, you have to find the answers to six basic questions: who, what, when, where, why, and how. The answers to these questions form part of the interviewing or interrogating package.

You must be a good listener, and you must listen with your ears, your eyes, and your heart. The fact that you are sitting quietly and listening does not necessarily mean that you understand what the subject has said. You have to listen in a two-dimensional manner. First, listen to the main point rather than the periphery. Many people become too interested in small details and do not pick up the main point of what is being said.

Second, evaluate what is being said by studying the subject's behaviour and manner of expression, the sound of his or her voice, and anything else connected with the subject's appearance. You should listen empathetically to understand the person and evaluate the testimony.

You are more likely to get a person to talk if you can develop some rapport. Before the interview, greet the person cordially, show respect, and find some common bond or interest. Don't necessarily start your interview with the main questions, but rather put the person at ease by talking about something you both share an interest in.

When interviewing, let the person tell his or her story— *uninterrupted*. Don't ask sudden questions. At the same time, do not allow any "dead points" in the conversation, or you will lose control. Don't ask questions that require only yes or no answers; otherwise, you end up doing most of the talking. Also, don't ask leading questions—they influence the answers you get.

Your last question should be something like: "What else do you think you can tell me?" or: "Is there anything I have not asked you that you thought I was going to ask you?" or: "Can you think of anything else?"

I find that a successful interview contains six elements, which I remember by making a mental checklist using the letters of the word "polite":

- Planning and preparation: Learn everything you can about the case beforehand, and jot down key questions.

- Opening remarks: Decide what it is you are going to say in the beginning, introduce yourself, and describe your credentials. Explain the purpose of the interview. Look for common interests, then develop rapport.

- Listening: Do not interrupt the subject. Learn to listen, but maintain eye contact and take your time.

- Interviewing: Keep your objective in mind. Obtain accurate information. Maintain control of the interview. Remember to ask who, what, when, where, why, and how.

- Thinking: Look for symptoms of deceit in the person's behaviour. Have you asked the key question? Have your objectives been met?

- Ending: End the interview in a courteous friendly manner. Shake hands with and thank the person. Summarize the interview for him or her. Make it easy for the subject to pass along other information to you by leaving your name and telephone number. Try to leave your subjects happy; if they like you, they'll call again.

In an interrogation, you take of course a completely different approach. The word conjures up visions of baseball bats, assault, and various forms of torture used in order to force the person to confess. Nothing could be further from the truth. The efficient interrogator has no need for violence and probably uses subtle, *psychological* pressures to pave the way for the person to confess to a crime.

Interrogating involves preparation—lots of it. Performing artists prepare themselves for their audiences; likewise, you must fine-tune your interrogation to suit the subject. Attempt to gain knowledge of the crime, the suspect, and your own abilities as an interrogator. Also, it's useful to prepare a "personality profile" of the person to help you phrase your questions. Here are some questions to ask yourself when preparing this profile:

- Who is your suspect? Make sure the full name is spelled correctly and that you can pronounce it properly, or else the suspect will think you know very little about him or her.

- What is the person's address? This may give you an indication of his or her socio-economic status.

- What is the person's age? A twenty-five-year-old interrogator may find it difficult to attack a fifty-year-old suspect by claiming greater experience.

- What is the person's occupation? This gives you an indication of how to talk to the suspect. You must be flexible enough to talk to a minister one minute and an illiterate ditchdigger the next.

- What is the suspect's work reputation? It can be helpful in inflating or deflating his or her ego during the interrogation. Using police liaison or public court records, attempt to find out if your suspect has a criminal record.

- What is the person's rank in the family? Try to find out if the person is the oldest or youngest sibling, and remember your own childhood experiences and where you stood in the family "pecking order."

- What is the person's ethnic background? The person may never look you in the eye because this is considered a sign of rudeness in his or her culture; so don't necessarily interpret it as a sign that the person is lying.

- What is the person's marital status? Is the spouse the dominant partner? Can you use the children to obtain a confession?

- What is the person's educational background? This give you information about his or her inclinations and way of thinking. There is a difference, for instance, between the way a student of law and a student of drama look at the world.

Never tell your subjects that you do not know what is going on or that their information is false. If you do, you destroy the reliability of the interrogation process.

To interrogate is to act. You must be flexible and have a variety of techniques to draw upon to obtain a confession. You must have a high level of perseverance and a low level of frustration; you must be able to laugh or cry at a moment's notice; you may have to appear religious or seem to know every dirty trick in the book.

Appearances are also important. Because we want to build relationships of authority and subordination during the interrogation, the interrogator must appear as an authoritative person. Do not enter the interrogation room wearing a T-shirt, blue jeans, and Adidas. A slightly conservative appearance can help a lot to create an impression of authority.

The setting for the interrogation should be carefully planned. The main factor that helps a suspect confess is privacy. There is an inner pressure to confide in someone, but usually in one person at a time and in a private setting. So your interrogation room must be isolated and free from interruptions of any kind, including phone calls.

Sit close to the person. This can create a great deal of anxiety, which is what you want. Try to speak the subject's language to prevent misunderstandings between you. But don't lessen your authority by using obscene or insulting expressions; authority requires self-respect and mutual respect.

The physical conditions of an interrogation room vary, of course, but, ideally, sit at a small desk in a small, windowless room. The desk should be in the corner of the room, and the subject's chair should be at a 90-degree angle to yours. The subject should sit with his or her back to the door. This type of set-up reduces distractions and creates intimacy and pressure.

Avoid a cluttered desk. Several files might encourage the suspect to waste time in the hope that you will go on to another case. One file can create the impression that the interrogator has lots of time to get the information.

Your desk should be clear of anything that might relieve the subject's tension. For example, removing ashtrays creates anxiety for the smoker. However, if the suspect has recently quit smoking, you may find that if you light up a cigarette the smoke may irritate his or her throat. Either way, tension is created that may lead to a quicker confession.

During the interrogation, always study body language. Look at the person's eyes: Are they shining or dimmed? Look at the mouth: Is it scowling or nervous? Follow the movement of the eyes and what direction they face. Look at the hands and legs: Does the suspect clench and unclench his or her fists? Does the person search for a place to put his or her hands? Does the person stand easily? Or does he or she shift the position of the legs every so often? The answers to these questions tell you how much tension the suspect is feeling.

Body language is always more noticeable when you grill the suspect with tough questions. For example, if a crime was committed at one a.m., and you ask firmly, "Where were you at one a.m.?" the person may show signs of being nervous, whether or not he or she is innocent. But if the person is guilty, the question should reveal the kinds of body language I have mentioned —beyond mere nervousness.

A Private Eye Tackles Information

In the world of private detective agencies, Intertel ranks near the top. It was established twenty years ago by some of the foremost intelligence people in the United States. Intertel's board of directors now includes the former heads of the National Security Agency, Scotland Yard, and the Royal Canadian Mounted Police.

The Canadian branch of Intertel was opened in 1971 by Calvin Hill, a former intelligence officer with the RCMP. Hill, who is now semi-retired, met the founders of Intertel while he was working in the U.S., on special loan from the Canadian government, to uncover organized crime. Intertel's directors were impressed with Hill, who had been with the RCMP for twenty-two years and had experience in many facets of criminal detective work, including planting bugging devices.

Surprisingly, Intertel acquires a lot of its information from public sources. And, as this interview with Hill reveals, a lot of information is acquired by using common sense approaches.

If we're hired to uncover how information has leaked from a company, we begin by drawing up a list of everyone who has had access to that information. We find out where the topic was formally discussed and who was present at the time. Because of my expertise with bugging devices, I may "sweep" the room with special equipment to detect any electronic devices that may have been planted. The occasional bug has been planted to gain access to company secrets, but this method is highly overrated. There's not nearly as much of it going on as you read about. What we do as a rule is simply interview everyone who had access to the information, and we often uncover a lot of employee indiscretion. This is especially true in high-tech companies where employees know specialists in other companies. The employees divulge confidential information—not intentionally—but sometimes to impress their friends.

But that's only one type of problem we're called in to solve. A company once hired us because they suspected an employee had been harassing another worker. A woman had been promoted over a male co-worker, and shortly afterward, strange things began to happen to her. She received obscene telephone calls, and her office dictionaries were ripped apart. The male colleague was suspected, but there wasn't any proof.

Our first move was to interview six employees who had good records and weren't suspects. We interviewed these workers because we didn't want anyone to know whom we suspected. We knew that once the interviews were over, they would talk to other employees. The workers didn't realize that we asked each of them a different set of questions, but we suspected that they would get together and come up with some common answers.

Then we brought in our suspect. He was shown into a large office and asked to sit in a particular chair that didn't have arms and was firmly planted, so he couldn't move around. I sat at my desk about 15 feet away, my hands folded comfortably in front of me. This arrangement unnerved him before any questions were asked.

My partner sat at another end of the room, and we began firing questions at the suspect from two directions, making him feel the pressure even more. I would ask one question, and before he finished answering, my partner would ask another. We had the man going back and forth like a yo-yo.

We deliberately discussed the good management of the firm and talked about its clever president. Because our suspect had been overlooked in the company and felt frustrated, we suspected that this type of discussion would disturb him. We kept on in this vein for about twenty minutes. Finally he blew up—he just couldn't restrain himself. Soon he told us about ripping up the dictionaries and then confessed to other things.

There are "softer" approaches to gathering information. It used to be that if there was a problem in a factory, we would plant an undercover agent to report to management, but that practice caused problems. We no longer use this approach, partly because of changing labour laws. If you're going to fire someone, you have to give him or her just cause, so you would have to disclose that you had planted an undercover person among the employees. That would trigger morale problems, and any new employee would be suspected of being an agent.

Our present method involves doing what we call "attitude surveys." We find they're far more productive than the under-cover approach and not as expensive. First, we announce on the general bulletin board that our firm has been brought in to examine the company. This notice asks for the co-operation of the workers.

Ninety percent of people are honest, but we have to give the company employee an "out" because of what we call the "rat-fink syndrome." Nobody wants to be thought a squealer. People may know what's going on in a company and disagree with it, and they may not be involved. But they don't want to disclose any information and therefore become involved. So we try to question people in such a way that we get the information we need without making them feel like informers.

For example, we've been hired to assess working conditions and morale inside a plant. We start by selecting the most junior person, say someone who has worked there for six months as a labourer. We ask him: "What would be the first thing you would do if you became the president of this firm?"

He may talk for an hour explaining what he would change and telling you things he sees going on in the plant all day. Perhaps he doesn't agree with many of them, but he is pleased to talk, because nobody has ever encouraged him to express his feelings before. And because we're outsiders, not the boss, he can open up.

If you select fifteen people from a staff of a hundred, you get a good insight into how that company is being run. In this cross-section will be several "retreads"—people who went to competing companies, then returned. These people are more likely to tell you what the sources of their problems have been.

We don't have any rigid guidelines for solving each case, but we usually start with a track sheet identifying the problem and the appropriate investigative sources. Sometimes a company hires us to investigate internal theft—an employee may be running a similar business after hours, on the side, and stealing company materials and tools. In addition to checking on the suspect's lifestyle to see if it's compatible with his or her salary, there are several sources we use.

We consult the Companies Services Branch of the Ontario Ministry of Consumer and Commericial Relations, which tells us if a company is registered, its address, the composition of its board of directors, and, in some cases, if it's taken out a loan. Local credit bureaus may yield personal financial information about the suspect. Dun & Bradstreet records may provide information about a company that the person in question is involved with. Newspaper clippings are an often overlooked source—they can be helpful for persons in the public eye. Court records can contain a wide range of information, including medical records and divorce settlements. Provincial land registry offices indicate land ownership. Voters' lists, available at any city hall, and city directories provide home addresses.

These sources can all be helpful. But quite often our information comes from interviewing neighbours. There is no set way to do this, but we normally knock on their doors and explain that we're inquiring about a person's financial situation. We approach neighbours in an informal way, and normally they co-operate, unless of course our suspect is in trouble with the law.

As you can see, there's no magic in uncovering information. There's no "Big Brother" handing us a file; it's really a matter of common sense. There is no one set way in which we operate. Instead, our approach is tailored to the particular problem. A case we solved using an unorthodox method involved a company that asked us to investigate one of their vice-presidents. We read through the executive's personnel file and noted he had an advanced degree from a particular university. We suspected this wasn't true.

To verify the information, we contacted the university but, as is often the case with educational institutions, it wouldn't tell us anything. Without any verification from the university we couldn't tell our client that the degree was fabricated; if the employee was fired but in fact had a degree, he could sue the firm for wrongful dismissal. We suggested to the company that their personnel department send a memo to all the executives stating that the department was updating their files and required copies of any diplomas. Everyone co-operated except the vice-president in question. He complained but finally admitted that he didn't hold the degree after all.

Looking Back: A Historian's Role

During an introductory course on Canadian history, 800 students cram into a University of Toronto classroom that seats only 200. The lecturer they are waiting to hear is the eminent historian J.M.S. Careless, whose numerous texts are required reading in high schools across Canada. Among the books he has written is a massive, two-volume biography of one of the founders of Confederation, George Brown. Brown of The Globe *won the Governor General's Award for non-fiction in 1962.*

In this conversation, Professor Careless explains how persistence paid off in acquiring the material for researching this biography. He also shares his approach to researching his latest project, an ambitious urban history of Canadian cities. Professor Careless believes a researcher must start his or her work by gaining general knowledge of a subject and then refining specific questions. He stresses critically evaluating sources for their importance and shows how to accomplish this.

I started my research for *Brown of The Globe* while I was doing my doctoral thesis at Harvard University. The thesis was actually a study called "Mid-Victorian Liberalism in a Colonial Environment" and was not a biography of George Brown. It really only captured his views as seen through the *Globe*. Rather than publish my thesis, I decided to expand it into a biography, but there was a problem of finding sources.

Very little had been written on Brown except the occasional book. The key for me was gaining access to the personal papers kept in the Brown family. Another Canadian historian, Frank Underhill, had tried to do this before me, in the 1930s. He had approached the only living son of Brown, George Mackenzie Brown, who was living in Scotland. Underhill had received very courteous letters, but the answer was always the same: the papers were personal family correspondence. Furthermore, George Mackenzie was considering writing a biography himself. I wrote to George Mackenzie myself during the Second World War and received the same reply.

Then, when I was giving a talk to a local historical society, I ran into Brown's grand-niece, Catherine Ball. She told me she had seen the papers in the family home in Scotland, and the material looked interesting. She encouraged me to approach the family again, because George Mackenzie had died and because she felt that his children wouldn't feel the same way about the material as their father had.

Such a change in attitude seems to be a common thing. A father is often viewed as a personal figure, almost sacrosanct, as in this case. But George Mackenzie's sons, who were then in their late fifties and sixties, didn't have these feelings about their grandfather. They had heard he was a noble character and thought it was great that someone should write his life story, but they didn't think there was anything of any significance in the papers.

I took a chance on the value of the material, received a grant, and went to Scotland. I found a trunk full of personal papers and a lot of political letters to Brown; other family members had said neither existed, but they were just at the bottom of the trunk. The personal letters were mostly written by Brown to his wife, and there was absolutely nothing in them that you would not have wanted to show to anyone then or now, because they contained his views of what was going on. His wife was a well-informed woman, and he was keeping her posted. I found letters that contained references to such things as John A. Macdonald coming into a cabinet meeting drunk again. It was very good material in every way. And it was much more than local colour—it was an inside view of Confederation by a man who was a major figure in it.

As is often the case, once I have this basic source, it leads to other sources. I found nothing of the same significance, but other material turned up because I had this lead, sometimes just by pure serendipity. For instance, material from the estate of former Liberal Prime Minister Alexander Mackenzie was suddenly turned over to Queen's University; it included correspondence between Brown and Mackenzie. This is the kind of development one learns of through the grapevine.

Sometimes it pays to advertise in newspapers and request information if you are researching someone who isn't well known. But everyone in the academic and historical community knew of Brown. I didn't need to advertise to trace his descendants, either, because an older family member had made the family history her life's hobby. She had stayed with the family in Scotland and painstakingly copied the birth and death entries from the parish register. She had even traced where the family members had moved. So I wrote to these people, who were still alive, and in some cases learned useful information about the family. This information must always be recognized as questionable, but if an individual is remembered by various people in the same way, it's probably true.

To organize my findings, I used five-by-eight-inch file cards. Each card was an item in itself, and I used both front and back if needed. The cards were colour-coded under different headings. In fact, when I was working on the book, I assembled a large suitcase full of cards. If the ship taking me home from Scotland had gone down, I would have jumped overboard with my suitcase, and to heck with everything else!

Right now I'm working on a major book that examines the external relations of Canadian cities. I cannot go into their internal affairs, except insofar as they influence external developments. No one has tried to synthesize the whole historical pattern of urban-regional development on a large scale, but I think it plays a large part in giving us the kind of Canada we now have. I'm calling the study "Metropolis and Frontier." It actually focuses on the nineteenth century, because I think that was our major era of frontier building.

I started the research for this book by reading the material already in print, although not everything in one fell swoop— there was far more than I needed. I had already been reading material on cities over the years, so a lot of the work was already done. This doesn't mean I didn't need to go back and reread what I thought I had remembered from this book or that, because I didn't necessarily have notes on the information. I didn't bother to make notes on the general books if I just wanted to refresh my memory on a topic I knew something about. I also gathered very good material from theses and students' research papers.

Then it was time to move to the primary research. There are a number of major depositories of material on Toronto; for example, the civic archives (at City Hall) keeps city council records and reports from various departments. This is true virtually all across the country.

The major libraries throughout Canada are also valuable resource centres. They usually have made some attempt to gather material on their own time. Here you can also find diaries and business records of local private individuals. Another useful source is provincial archives, the holdings of which usually predate those of civic archives. Provincial archives often also stores family papers.

In addition to these sources, there is the National Archives of Canada in Ottawa. You can find masses of material there for filling in gaps. For instance, Board of Trade papers might be incomplete in one city, but you may pick up missing volumes in the National Archives. There are also many private papers there on cities.

If you want to go beyond that in dealing with the internal history of a city, labour records are helpful. For instance, in Toronto I used material from the Typographical Union.

What you must do in research, in any case, is work from the general to the particular. That involves first orienting yourself. The mistake a lot of beginners make is to approach their subject too specifically, by looking up a published item on a particular place in a particular district, for example. They go immediately to the wider and primary data; maybe they get beyond it, or maybe they don't. Perhaps they want to research the life of a person; again they go to a library and ask: "What have you got specifically on that individual?"

Very often a helpful librarian can take you a long way on such questions. But more often beginners simply search out the articles or books by the titles and don't know enough about the subject to ask themselves what the critical inquiries are that need pursuing. Try to orient yourself about your subject *before* you go after the specific questions. This means, in historians' terms, scanning and comprehending the secondary sources available. Find what is useful in print. Once you already know something about the topic, you have a kind of grid in your mind that lets you say,"Well, I can screen this out, and I don't really need that. This is too general, or that's not the part that I want to cover."

Even a historian who supposedly knows a good deal about a historical event or person almost automatically starts by reading biographies (or even newspaper accounts) before zeroing in on the particulars. I repeat: don't go to your primary, specific material until you cover the general.

In research, you have to establish a mental pattern of critical evaluation. I don't mean that you set up a neat, one-to-ten scale. But in your mind you start thinking that way. It is both common sense and also simply inevitable, once you begin to know something about the subject. You don't just say: "This is more significant than that." You are really asking: "How valid does this seem to me in forwarding my inquiry?" It's fair to add that you can't do much better than express this as *"seem* to me." One can proclaim a great deal about being objective and above bias, and it *is* important to try. But what you're finally saying is: "In my opinion (or in my now-informed judgement) this is the way I would rate this authority's material." The more you know about the subject, the more convincingly you can do it.

There are some common rules for this process of evaluation. For instance, the closer to an event the source record was made, the more likely it is to be valid. People are more likely to remember accurately what happened during or soon after an event than they are reminiscing about it fifty years later.

On the other hand, one must also take into consideration that when a source describes an event immediately or soon after, they may not have very much perspective on it. It may even be wrong about what happened. Consider our newspapers. They report that so-and-so got his head bashed in by so-and-so at four a.m.; well, it may be so, and it may not. They might print two days later: "Sorry, folks; it was three-thirty, and it wasn't him at all, and it was two other guys who did it."

This is human and natural, but it shows that against the immediacy of the source, you have to appraise the quality of information the source is likely to have. One way to judge this is by cross-testing: compare one source against another, if you're lucky enough to have a variety. Then you can form your best judgement. It won't be the perfect judgement, but it will be the best one you can make on the basis of your most complete information.

A Cabinet Minister's Approach

Frank Drea's researching talents began to surface when he was an undergraduate student, and he graduated from Buffalo's Canisius College cum laude. With his high scholastic aptitude, he seemed destined to become a university professor. Instead, he became a journalist and eventually an Ontario cabinet minister.

Drea was once an investigative labour reporter for the now-defunct Toronto Telegram, *and it was there that he gained notoriety as an astute and relentless reporter with a penchant for uncovering corruption. His work was so widely recognized that the CBC created a half-hour dramatic television series, "McQueen," based on Drea's life.*

At the Telegram *Drea created North America's first "Action Line" newspaper column, investigating consumer complaints. It was the prototype for many others.*

He also wrote a series of front-page articles about five Italian labourers who were killed in a tunnel collapse on a sewer construction project in North Toronto in 1960. The articles were brilliantly researched and revealed several underlying issues: Italian labourers were being brutally exploited; safety regulations were being ignored; and the construction companies were getting kickbacks and evading income tax. The series resulted in a Royal Commission, the findings of which led to the tightening up of industrial safety legislation in Ontario, a more rigid system of inspection, the formation of trade union locals, and new minimum-wage laws. Drea was awarded the prestigious Heywood Broun Award for the articles—the first time a Canadian had ever won the honour. This is an American award usually bestowed upon such publications as the New York Times.

In this candid interview, he reflects on how he researched the tunnel disaster. Most of his information came from speaking directly with the workers and from carefully reading the legislation involved.

Drea, a former Minister of Consumer and Commercial Relations, also explores a few ways to gather information on companies.

There is always a reason *why* things are done. Once you understand the "why," you can make some sense out of a situation. You don't have to be an industrial engineer to investigate an industrial accident, but you can't investigate anything unless you understand some of the background. The real key to researching the Hogg's Hollow tunnel story was to talk to the workers themselves.

Briefly stated, the initial story was about a private company which had been contracted by Metro Toronto to install a tunnel under a section of the Don River. The company encountered quicksand and other impediments that hadn't been expected in the area. As a result, it decided to use much higher air pressure than usual to keep these impediments out while the labourers worked below. The tragedy began when a few of the men began to smoke. That caused a fire, which burned the insulation off the air hoses; the smoke overcame most of them. To worsen the situation, someone above turned off the air pressure, thinking that this would kill the fire and smoke. But the moment this was done the Don River came crashing in, along with tons of sand and dirt. Five of the six men were killed instantly.

The story originally came to my attention when another labourer on the project walked into the *Telegram* office, asking to see a reporter. He had quit his job because of what he said were unsafe working conditions. So I had his allegation to start with.

The first thing to understand when beginning this type of research is that someone is in charge of the work site. So I asked myself: "What did this person (or persons) do or not do that allowed this to happen?" An accident like this occurs very rarely, so I also asked myself: "Was everything that was designed to prevent this kind of thing from happening functioning properly? Were there any safety regulations that applied in this situation, and were they followed?" In other words, I looked at this case the way a police officer would: there were five deaths in an industrial accident, and I wanted to know what caused the accident.

At that time, Ontario had great legislation covering trench work, but no one ever enforced it. ("Trench work" means installing sanitary and storm sewers.) The unwritten agreement was that the government didn't have to enforce it, because the union's business agent would do it. But when this type of work was done outside of downtown Toronto, the unions weren't involved. It was the newly-landed Italian immigrants who worked the suburbs; they couldn't work downtown, because they couldn't pass the screening exams, which were all in English. And as I learned from talking with these labourers, *anything* went on in the suburban areas.

I spent a little time gathering existing public records. Because this was a construction project, a building permit had had to be filed with the provincial government. This was public information. I wanted to see this permit, because I wanted to know who had approved the building plans. The permit told me that the Department of Labour, as it was then called, had done so on the basis of a submission filed by a person who claimed he was an engineer.

I checked out the engineer's credentials by calling the Association of Professional Engineers. It turned out that the man wasn't a registered engineer after all. That information opened up other avenues for me.

I also carefully read the department's Tunnel Regulations, which regulated underground work using compressed air. After interviewing various union officials, I learned that there was a printing error in the law. The word "minimum" had been used instead of "maximum"—if the labourers had followed the regulations to the letter, *every* worker would have died.

As is the case with any construction project, inspection reports had had to be filed with the Department of Labour. By reading these public documents, I found out that a government inspector had gone to the site but hadn't actually *inspected* the work being done. The report simply said he had *visited* the site, not inspected it. I probed a little further to find out why this was so. It turned out that there was only one department inspector for this type of work. He was about to retire, and because he had a heart condition, his doctor had forbidden him to go anywhere where there was air pressure. Everyone in the department knew this; it was no secret.

By this point my research, which was far from over, had revealed that this was a real "bucketshop" operation—really "Mickey Mouse."

The one worker who had escaped the disaster was a middle-aged Polish man who had survived cave-ins in Europe as a prisoner during the Second World War. He knew how to get out. But after this last close call, he went on a drinking binge for a week. No one knew where he was. A fellow employee gave me his address, and I waited outside his house for three nights in a row, from midnight until five in the morning. He eventually showed up, of course, and spoke with me, confirming the original allegation that the working conditions were far from safe on this job.

If I were researching this story today, some of the information would be easier to retrieve. I could get the building plans instantly from the Building Department at Toronto City Hall. The inspection reports mentioned earlier would be posted on the job site and filed with what is now the provincial Ministry of Labour. And using a word processor at the Workers' Compensation Board, I could quickly get a printout of the occupational health and safety record of any company. Even probing legislation would be easier today. You can visit the Ontario Government Bookstore on Bay Street and quickly purchase a copy of any legislation. When I was working on this story, I had to line up for hours on York Street.

While doing the research on the tunnel tragedy, other interesting information came my way. The workers told me that, on average, one Italian labourer was killed each month while working in the trenches in the suburbs. The provincial safety regulations required lumber to be used as bracing for this work and protective helmets to be worn. But this equipment was not used, because it was an additional expense for the employers. This was a clear contravention of the safety regulations. To follow up these allegations, I attended several inquests into the deaths of trench workers. I discovered a pattern: at the inquests, the fire department would say there was no lumber present when they dug up the dead worker. But a lawyer would always produce photographs of lumber sticking out of the ground; the lawyer would swear that there was so much lumber, they would have to burn it. This was nothing less than a cover-up. Clearly, no one was enforcing the safety requirements, at least not in the suburban areas.

My research was beginning to paint an ugly picture. It showed that there were actually two worlds in Ontario: one for people who were born in this country, the other for Italian immigrants.

I learned of these atrocities by interviewing the people other reporters wouldn't talk to. There were 10,000 Italian labourers in the Toronto area then; most of them were newly arrived from Italy and didn't speak English very well. Ironically, they came from a society advanced in industrial safety, while here in Canada they were being ruthlessly exploited. Contractors went so far as to hold back ten to twenty percent of their wages; when the workers asked their bosses why, they were told it was to pay for the Queen's jewels! They would be shown a picture of the Queen and told: "She has a crown, right? Okay, you came to Canada, pal. She's our Queen, right? Okay, you pay ten percent." The poor labourer paid an illegal tax on his wages, and the employer who skimmed it from his paycheque paid nothing. It was unbelievable what went on. And this startling information came to me by simply talking to these men— it was that easy.

When I was a reporter in the 1960s, the approaches to gathering information were slightly different. It was novel to have women gathering information, for example, because women had never worked in this milieu. A newspaper might hire an actress to interview someone and have her wear a hidden "body pack" tape recorder. Bugging devices were also used. But today these approaches are obsolete; we live in a much more sophisticated age. There is a great body of information available that wasn't available then.

For example, if you want to research a company today, your starting point is to obtain a copy of its registration from the provincial Ministry of Consumer and Commercial Relations.*

---

* *Author's note:* Refer to Chapters 13, 14 and 15 on government sources for further information.

This gives you the address of the company and the names and addresses of its directors—information that is easily available to the public.

But don't think that a registration check spells out all the details and any wrongdoings of a company. And don't feel that because a company is registered with the government, the province has given it its blessing. Neither of these assumptions is correct. The function of registration records is to give an address where the company's executives can be served with a summons in case of a lawsuit—that's all.

A brief word on numbered companies: some people believe that numbered companies are sinister, but the only reason there are numbered companies is that the English language wasn't keeping pace with incorporations. Business people were being prevented from forming companies because they couldn't name them fast enough. Remember the old letter prefixes in our telephone numbers? Bell Canada changed from letter prefixes to numerical prefixes for reasons of efficiency.

It's easy to collect financial information on public companies. Their earnings are listed in several places, including the *Card Index*, published by The Financial Post's Corporation Service Group and available in the public library. Or you can call any brokerage house and ask for the information, saying that you're interested in buying shares in the company. Also, the public has access to provincial records in provincial securities commission files.

Another, often overlooked, source of information on companies is the municipality where they are located. Municipalities are revenue collectors and therefore keep all sorts of business licences or permits that you can ask to see. When companies file information with the provincial and federal governments, they usually have a lawyer fill out the forms carefully. But when they're filing information with a municipality, the owners of the company generally do so themselves and are much more open about their affairs.

Very few people ask to see another type of public record—tax assessment rolls. These are never more than five or six months out of date because, in Ontario at least, they're tied to the enumeration system for municipal elections. Tax assessment rolls are kept in city hall archives and are a great source when trying to locate a person or determine what a company's property is worth.

Court records can be beneficial as well. You can use them to discover if there are any judgements against an individual or a company, if an action was contested, and if there have been any bankruptcies.

Determining land ownership is easy enough to do. There are massive land registry systems in each province that the public can use to trace any piece of land back hundreds of years.

Gaining financial information on private companies is tricky, but there are a few sources that are helpful. When private companies borrow money, they first have to establish credibility; to do this, they usually co-operate with financial clearing houses. For a relatively small fee, you can check a company's credit rating, which, because records must be kept up-to-date, can yield a lot of information. There are various specialized clearing houses that provide this service; it depends on the industry you're investigating.

As you can see, there is in fact a lot of information on the public record: there's no need to count on stumbling onto things the way we used to. When I was a reporter, there wasn't the record-keeping system that exists today. In a way, there's too much information available now. In order to get down to the bone, you have to discard 99 percent of the information you obtain. It's really the 1 percent you're after: the "why" of things. Everything else then falls into place.

Researching Fiction

Timothy Findley's novels are meticulously researched. Even his publisher's lawyers admit to having difficulty determining where fact ends and fiction begins.

Famous Last Words, Findley's fourth and most exhaustively prepared book, required four years of research. A gripping account of fascism during the Second World War, the novel probes an international cabal whose members include the Duke and Duchess of Windsor, prominent Nazis, and other well-known figures. The narrator is Hugh Mauberley, a fictitious figure borrowed from one of Ezra Pound's poems. Mauberley is an American expatriate writer who is a confidant of members of the cabal. He knows too much, flees the Nazis, hides in an Austrian hotel, and scrawls everything he knows in silver pencil along the walls of the hotel. He is murdered while doing this, and the story really unfolds by flashing back to his handwritten account.

In the following interview, Findley reveals how relatively simple the research was for this complex novel.

At a writer's conference, I had a wonderful talk with the author E.L. Doctorow. He wrote what I would call the definitive metafiction book, *Ragtime*. When I asked him how he did his research, he answered this way: "I discovered that once I had really stated my subject, I became a magnet." That is a very good definition of what happens when you have staked out your territory. Doctorow's territory was pre-First World War. My territory was 1943 back to wherever it was going to lead as far as the Duke and Duchess of Windsor were concerned.

The magnet phenomenon works as follows: you pick up a book of basic history, you read, and you discover a sequence of names. Let us pretend that Doctorow and I have picked up the same book. Doctorow does not write or think like me, and I do not write or think like him; therefore, he and I are not going to follow the same line in reading this book. As Doctorow reads— and this is the magnet at work—his eye hits on a particular sequence, and he follows it. He picks up on names, personality traits, the recurrence of links between people and events. A whole other set of magnetic episodes are going to happen with me.

My subject dictated a sequence that followed fascist thinking from one set of people to another. I had to begin with something basic, so I used W.L. Shirer's *Rise and Fall of the Third Reich*—an invaluable guide to fascism and the Second World War. Where did it take me? For one thing, its bibliography gave me a reading list. I discovered an alarming consistency in the cast of characters from one piece of reading to another. Here's a good example: in one book I discovered that the wedding of the Duke and Duchess of Windsor had taken place at the Château du Conde in France, which was owned by a man named Charles Eugène Bedaux. The information was a mere mention of the wedding—just a sentence—but I had never heard of Bedaux and was intrigued. In another book, however, I had read that prior to the wedding the Duchess was staying with friends in their villa in the south of France and the Duke was with friends at a castle in Austria. That led to the question, "Why did they get married at Bedaux's villa—seemingly, the home of a stranger—when they could have been married where they already had friends whom they knew were willing to perform the ceremony?"

Reading newspaper accounts of the wedding, I learned that Bedaux had offered the Windsors his villa absolutely out of the blue—he did not even know them. And I still knew very little about him; he was a mystery and a challenge. What helped me understand this man was a series of columns written by Janet Flanner in the *New Yorker*. Sure enough, my instinct had been correct. I had made the right connection, and Bedaux had been worth tracking, because it turned out that he had been pivotal to the Windsors' fascist connections.

Bedaux was the inventor of the concept of *time study*. He would walk into factories and say, "Get rid of those people— they're stopping you. Bring in other people and make use of them." He worked out a system that to me is highly fascist: he would extract the most from labourers, making them work very hard for four minutes, then relax for one minute. In other words, he advocated turning people into machines to make them more productive. The carrot to reward them was the one minute of rest. He made a fortune. And, not incidentally, some Canadian firms adopted his methods.

I read through all the books I could find on the Windsors to discover any further connections with Bedaux. I had to do a lot of scrutinizing, because some books were very sympathetic and others were overly damning. A good researcher has to learn to recognize an author's bias.

The real starting point for me was to determine what was to be the circle of events and who were to be the people involved in this cabal I was imagining—and then to discover what might have been real. By reading through material I had borrowed from libraries and purchased at bookstores, I discovered that at its widest, the circle included people like Ezra Pound, the Duke and Duchess of Windsor, Bedaux, Walter Schellenberg (who was the top SS counterintelligence officer), Ribbentrop, and Rudolf Hess. The magnet in me took over once I had that overview. As soon as I saw any of those names, I would mentally reach out to collect data. I could be walking down the street and out of the corner of my eye see Hess's face staring out of a bookstore window from the dust jacket of a book. It's an eclectic process.

I also read the *bibliographies* of every book I used and followed them up, ultimately reading nearly everything written about some of these key figures. By reading and rereading material I acquired, over time, a deeper understanding of the characters I had found.

Another thing that paid off for me was to tell friends what I was writing about. One of these friends, the writer Charles Taylor, was especially helpful. His father, E.P. Taylor, lives in Nassau, and the Taylors inevitably got to know some of the people in the circle around the Duke of Windsor during his tenure there as governor during the Second World War. This connection turned out to be invaluable for me. In my novel I used a real-life incident involving Sydney Oakes and his father, Sir Harry Oakes, but I gave my own interpretation of the circumstances in which it had taken place. It is a pertinent scene that develops the character of Sir Harry and, I think, forms a part, however small, of the explanation of why he was murdered.

When I had finished *Famous Last Words*, the lawyers for my publisher, Clarke Irwin, were worried that Sydney might still be alive and sue. My memory told me he had died in a car accident. Charles Taylor helped me confirm this by telephoning his father's secretary in Nassau. The secretary made a few calls to relatives of the Oakeses, who confirmed that, indeed, he was dead.

There were other areas where Charles Taylor helped me. A number of places mentioned in my book—Spain, Vienna, Rome, Venice, and Nassau—were places I had never been. Quite deliberately, I avoided visiting them, because I wanted to maintain a kind of mythic view of them, so that they would be "written" places, not real. I read a lot about them and asked a lot of questions. For instance, I mentioned to Charles Taylor that I had placed the governor's mansion in Nassau at the top of a hill. He remarked, "Yes, it's at the top of a sort of hill. It's actually just a slight rise in the land." He was greatly amused. I also asked him other questions: "What do the trees smell like?" "What does the land smell like at night?" By researching the setting in this way, I was getting a mythic, distanced, very "writerly" interpretation of the place. Don't forget: the book was being written by a writer, Mauberley, who was a failed romantic. I had to serve his style.

I also studied maps in the library to get the geography and street connections right. Studying the photographs was also helpful to make sure I was correctly describing the clothing, cars, and things like that. There were the kinds of details Mauberley thrived on: dress, appearance, atmosphere.

This process is, of course, different than a journalistic reportage of a place. That is a valid type of approach, but it would destroy a book like mine, which requires a different kind of shape to make it succeed.

I didn't do all the research in one fell swoop. I would research, then write, then repeat the process. I might suddenly say to myself, "Okay, now I need everything I can get about Ezra Pound," then plunge into that and place the material into my Pound file.

I used four filing boxes for my novel, each of them measuring two-and-a-half-feet deep. I would file material under names, places, clothing, photographic material, and songs.

Songs were very important. I had to find the words to various songs, and that's not as easy as it might appear. There is a moment in *Famous Last Words* when Edward and Mrs. Simpson are experiencing the sort of romance where they have to hold hands under the table. They couldn't touch one another openly, because the whole world was staring. I thought it was appropriate to have music in the background that would recreate the atmosphere of this scene. I cross-referenced songs at a special library at the Canadian Broadcasting Corporation and came up with Jerome Kern's 1936 hit, "A Fine Romance," with the words, ". . . A fine romance, my friend, this is; a fine romance, with no kisses . . ." Perfect.

I never made a trip to the reference library in Toronto to research just one point. I would make a list of ten points to research, and this made the trip worthwhile.

You have to be very careful when you research a novel. I made a few embarrassing mistakes. For one thing, I created a non-existent rank in the Royal Air Force. Somebody picked it up early enough, so that by the time the book was published in the United States, it had been corrected.

Here's a story to explain how I could have avoided a few other major errors. Every year in mid-August, I visit a wonderful old hotel along the coast of Maine. Some very interesting people stay there. On this particular visit, I met an English-woman, Diana Marler, and told her about my novel, which was then in progress. She told me that her best friend was the daughter of Sir Edward Peacock, who had been the Duke of Windsor's lawyer. Diana even had a desk that Peacock had once owned and that the Duke himself had used when signing legal papers.

I lent Diana all of the manuscript dealing with Ned Allenby, whom I had created as the British Undersecretary of State for Foreign Affairs. The Allenby home is set in Kent, England, where Charles Lindbergh turns up and Allenby is murdered. I had, in fact, made Allenby up by modelling him on a conglomerate of several people, some of them well known. The portrait of Allenby was apparently so effective that people told me after they had read the book that they had known him! Some had even known him "very well."

Diana Marler told me she had found two *glaring* mistakes. I was alarmed. The first one concerned a scene I had written in which a gardener is pushing a wheelbarrow full of dead marigolds. She pointed out that people of Allenby's station would never have grown marigolds—marigolds were "cottage" flowers. My flowers would have to be some other kind, like roses. That may sound silly, but it was terribly important. The garden had to be right; it was key material.

She also pointed out where I had used an improper phrase. In the scene where Lindbergh is trying to sell Allenby on fascism and the Nazis, Allenby becomes so angry that he says: "I don't want to hear about this, you goddamn son of a bitch." Diana said Allenby would never have used the term "son of a bitch." He might have called Lindbergh a bloody idiot, or a bastard, but no Englishman of that class would have used the North American term I had given him. Like a fool I said, "Thank you, Diana, I'll think about that." I though that "bastard" wasn't strong enough and left my original term in.

I shouldn't have. A dozen people have come up to me since the book was published and told me, "I really loved the book, but—in *England*—why did Ned Allenby call Lindbergh a son of a bitch? He would never have said that." Readers pick up on these things, and Diana was right. It sounds almost trite, but, you see, it isn't; using the wrong phrase destroyed the veracity of that scene.

The lesson here is that you have to learn to be a good listener. Your will has to bow to the research, and you have to accommodate information. I didn't, and it had a jarring effect on a significant number of readers. They lost the thread of the moment when they read that sentence and thought, "Oh, that's wrong!"

Coming back to where I began, the personality searching for any given information dictates how that research proceeds. If you handed five writers the same subject and said, "All five of you are going to research and write about this topic," they would write five totally different books. This is so because each writer has his or her own magnet, a completely unique way of interpreting things, guided by personal imagination.

Tracing Ancestors

For twenty-four years, Hugh MacMillan's official title was "Archives Liaison Officer" for the Public Archives of Ontario. The title hardly reflected the job which MacMillan had created for himself—being a full-time manuscript sleuth. One national magazine referred to him as "history's super snoop [who] tracks archival treasures with the fervour of a big-game hunter." Laurentian University recognized his talents by awarding him an honorary Doctor of Letters degree.

In this interview MacMillan recalls two of the hundreds of cases he has solved and concludes by offering researchers tips on doing their own genealogical research.

My job involves *reverse genealogy*. Most people engage in genealogical research to trace their family history, starting with themselves and working backwards. I start with a historical figure and work forward to locate living descendants.

Reverse genealogy is fraught with many frustrations and false trails. It starts with choosing a historical figure (which could, of course, be your ancestor) whose papers may still be out there somewhere. The next step is to assemble known genealogical data and commence a family tree, working from the historical figure down to living descendants.

Let's take a few examples of cases I have worked on. The first involves one small part of my own family tree, the research for which overlapped into my professional life. I had worked out a great deal of my MacMillan family tree (using approaches which I will refer to at the end of the two examples) and discovered that my great-great-grandmother, Margaret Grant, was a cousin of a fur trader, Alexander Grant. Since fur trading was a major industry in Ontario in the latter part of the eighteenth century and early nineteenth century, *any* fur trader's papers were of historical interest. Thus I was able to focus on tracking down Alexander Grant's papers for my employer, the Ontario Archives. This one assignment will give you some idea of how one tiny aspect of genealogical research can turn out.

The research began by contacting my cousin, Duncan Grant, in Glengarry, Ontario. Like me, he was interested in the Grant connection but had not researched it. Still, he was helpful insofar as he referred me to another relative, Mildred Grant, in Portland, Oregon. These continuous referrals should not discourage you. You will find yourself being referred by one relative to another, from one city or province or country to another, and so forth. This is part of genealogical research. The idea is to locate a relative who has already done some of the research. This way you avoid having to do everything yourself.

Mildred Grant provided me with various information, but the most important thing was her referral to Grace Mitchell, another descendant of Grant, who lived in Victoria, British Columbia. As is the case in most of my research, I visited this relative in person. Personal visits often yield the best results. Grace was the kind of source that saves any researcher a lot of work. A lively, talkative, eighty-year-old self-appointed family historian, she had collected portraits of Alexander Grant and his wife and a lot of their family papers, too.

Grace had shipped all of her research in a large chest to her cousin, Gordon Urquhart. Urquhart lived in Montreal, Quebec, but Grace had lost contact with him. She had an old address, however, and I took note of this.

When I was in Montreal I looked up this address and interviewed neighbours and the landlord. I discovered from the landlord that Urquhart was still renting a parking space for his decrepit Jaguar. He kept a green chestnut canoe on top of the car and once a year travelled to this address, paid for a year's

worth of parking and took a brief fishing trip in the Lauren-
tians. The landlord and neighbours did not have a current
address for Urquhart.

By this point I had carefully searched through the telephone
book, consulted directory assistance for new telephone listings
and city directories, and looked at other potential leads but
could not locate Urquhart. My only alternative was to leave a
detailed note pinned to his canoe, urging him to contact a
lawyer friend of mine in Montreal.

My approach worked. The lawyer heard from Urquhart, and
I returned to Montreal in a hurry to interview this descendant.
It was then I learned the bad news. Two years earlier, there had
been a fire in the old Crescent Arms apartment building he
lived in, and all of his belongings were destroyed. Unfortunately, these included the papers I was after. No copies had
been made—a mistake no genealogist should make.

In this case I had arrived too late and was forced to close the
file. One more loser, but the "law of averages" would see to it
that the next case or maybe the one after that would be a winner! Should you meet a similar dead end in your chase, it might
seem best, at that point, to drop the matter. Still, it is as well to
keep the case on file as the finale to the Grant case illustrates.

Ten years later, on a canoe trip, my companions and I made a
stopover at Duldreggan Hall, which is situated on the Ottawa
River at L'Original, near Hawkesbury, Ontario. This was the
house that Alexander Grant retired to in about 1802. The
owners of this unofficial historical site, Betty and Drummond
Smith, are friends of mine. Betty took me aside to pass on some
exciting news. A police detective had contacted them recently
about a collection of early nineteenth century letters addressed
to, "Alexander Grant, Esq., Duldreggan Hall, L'Original, Upper
Canada." The police had made some inquiries and eventually
located the Smiths.

The papers had been found when the police raided the premises of local burglars. It turned out that these same thieves had
stolen the papers from Gordon Urquhart's apartment. The
police believed that the thieves had torched the building to
cover their thefts.

The sequel to this case illustrates the need to maintain a
healthy degree of optimism in this line of research. You hear
a lot of things that appear far-fetched, and you may feel you are
embarking on a wild goose chase. But if there is a glimmer of
hope, it is worth following up on a lead. This is a chancy

business to begin with, and thus it is not good to give up easily. My next case illustrates this even further.

The *Toronto Telegram* once ran a story about what I do for a living, and this drew a series of letters and telephone calls. One of these was from a Toronto lady; I'll refer to her as Mrs. T. in this anecdote. She claimed she had the gold snuff box that had belonged to Mary, Queen of Scots, other objects belonging to Scottish royalty, an assortment of Jacobite portraits and a set of pistols that had belonged to James Edgar, secretary to King James of Scotland. The story seemed highly improbable but grabbed my interest because a collateral descendant, Sir James Edgar, had been the Speaker in the House of Commons under Sir Wilfrid Laurier, and I wondered whether any of Sir James's papers might be traced through this lead.

Mrs. T. said the items belonged to a friend with whom she had lost contact. She now found that she had to dispose of the items because the government was expropriating her house for a local development.

I agreed to meet her in a month. In the interim, her friend's son surfaced and claimed most of the objects. That didn't disturb me, as my real interest was not in the Scottish relics but in any historical papers that had belonged to Sir James Edgar.

My visit to Mrs. T. was more fruitful than the telephone call had been. The lady was kind enough to let me assist her in searching the house for any of Edgar's personal papers. I thought I was thorough but found nothing. I left my business card on the off chance that something might turn up later. It is always a good practice to leave a card and make follow-up calls. This keeps all parties interested in the case. It is also a good idea to keep a file on who you have contacted and when because seemingly unrelated bits of information might very well lead to a complete picture down the road.

My next step was tracing the son of Sir James Edgar, David Edgar. Mrs. T. had told me he was a war veteran, so, I approached government officials in charge of pension records, hoping to secure an address. As a rule, this isn't public information, although they may assist relatives. In my own case, working on behalf of a government tracing historical papers, I was assisted. The address provided, however, was badly out of date. However, through the use of city directories in the public library, I eventually traced him. I did this by looking up his old address and taking note of former neighbours. One telephone call led to another, until I located him.

David Edgar was living in a dilapidated rooming house in downtown Toronto and agreed to see me. Unfortunately, he didn't have his family papers. Still, the contact was an important one since he assisted me in compiling a family tree of the Edgar family. He provided me with some names and addresses of family members. I was able to find further addresses by using, once again, city directories in the public library. I then began the long task of contacting Edgar's relatives, who were scattered from Peterborough to Victoria.

About a year after I began this case, I received a telephone call from the daughter of Mrs. T.'s housekeeper. Mrs. T. had moved out and offered free rent to her housekeeper's daughter until the building's demolition. The housekeeper's daughter had made an important discovery. In some boxes destined for the garbage, she had found a black tin box and, upon opening it, discovered a batch of old papers. She threw the papers in the garbage outside and kept the box. That night it rained, and winds scattered the papers across the yard. The next day she retrieved the papers to place them in the garbage and noticed early nineteenth century postmarks. She remembered my visit the year before and found my number. This turned out to be a good example of the value of a business card. The papers turned out to be significant political and personal papers of Sir James Edgar. The Ontario Archives rewarded her for taking the trouble to contact us.

Sometimes luck seems to play a role in obtaining leads, although it is still necessary to follow up on all leads. This was the case with the sequel to the Edgar project. It will be the same with your research. No lead is too trivial; check them all out.

Another year had elapsed since I had secured Sir James Edgar's papers. I was on a canoe trip near James Bay working on a film about the Hudson's Bay Company. Suddenly we hit a number of huge rocks in a long stretch of rapids and broke twenty-two ribs of our canoe. Fate, it seemed, had taken a hand in my search! We were forced to abandon our trip at Moose River crossing. We waited there for five hours for a train. As we were waiting, two young women appeared. They were local school teachers, and they invited us into their log cabin for dinner. Betsy Wood, one of the two, asked me what I did for a living. Upon hearing that I located and acquired historical documents, she suggested I visit her mother in Huntsville, Ontario.

Betsy's mother's maiden name was Edgar! She was one of

the cousins I had attempted to locate, and she had another collection of Edgar papers! She also put me in touch with her first cousin in Toronto, a lead I did not have. This cousin had even more of Edgar's papers. So the chase went on.

You can look forward to some variation of the Grant or Edgar cases in your own search. To aid you in your genealogical research I offer the following light rules and precepts. These have helped me in constructing my own family tree. Enjoy the search; it will be frustrating, but fun.

- Join the nearest genealogical society, as it may save you endless searching, particularly if it turns out that some other relative has been working on your family line.

- Check in your local library for a basic handbook on genealogical research. Borrow, or better still, buy a copy; then follow its precepts.

- Assemble all known information about your ancestor in question and record birth dates and places of residence. There are very productive sources that will assist you in this, including assessment rolls, church records, and census returns.

- Examine maps covering the area where your ancestor lived.

- Record the information you find in an orderly manner, so it can be made use of in your published family history.

- Contact all known descendants to assemble and record anecdotes, biographical data, and photographs. This is guaranteed to make your family history much more informative and entertaining. Nothing is duller than a bare genealogical chart.

- Assemble a name list of all known descendants. This will take time, and all descendants you know should be asked to give names of descendants they know. A home computer is preferable, but not absolutely essential.

- Having gone to all of this work, you should investigate the costs of printing or desktop publishing to produce your book. Once you have done this write a letter to all of your descendants with a synopsis of your work. With proper planning you should be able to sell the book ahead of time and recover all costs.

CHAPTER
9

Library Research

Brian Land is one of Canada's most outstanding librarians. He headed the Business and Industry Division of the Windsor Public Library before becoming executive assistant to the federal Minister of Finance in 1963. He has been a professor in the Faculty of Library Science at the University of Toronto and its Dean, as well as the president of the Canadian Library Association. The author of an invaluable research tool, Directory of Associations in Canada, *Land has been the executive director of the Ontario Legislative Library since 1978.*

In this account he discusses basic approaches to using libraries in Canada.

The first thing for a researcher to do is to identify, as closely as possible, what the problem is. Most library users are notoriously vague about what they want, so they must first understand what the search is supposed to accomplish. To achieve this, it is helpful to find out what the application or context of the information might be; one way to do this is to narrow down the geographical area of the search. For example, if information on gardening is requested, the geographical aspect is espe-

62

cially important, because information must be appropriately selected for different terrains. The time frame of the material you seek is another way to refine questions.

It is useful to skim through a book, article, or a library's clipping file on a subject to gain an overview of your material. This process may make you change the direction of your research, because as you learn something about the subject in general, you may become fascinated with certain aspects of it. This approach also helps you refine and define your questions.

It helps to distinguish between the different kinds of information available. A student writing a high school paper might find an essay in an encyclopedia an appropriate source. On the other hand, someone preparing an article for a learned journal would require academic sources as opposed to more popular information.

Indexes are extremely valuable in any kind of library research, and yet I have found that even first-year university students are unaware of the most standard periodical indexes. The most basic periodical indexes in our country are the *Canadian Periodical Index*, the *Canadian News Index*, the *Canadian Business Index*, *Canadian Magazine Index*, and the *Microlog Index*. They cover most Canadian newspapers, magazines, journals, and government and business reports.*

Indexes are being offered increasingly through on-line computer services. But computerization really only started in the late 1960s, which means that you still have to do manual index searches if you wish to locate publications before this period. There are directories that tell you if a particular publication has been indexed, the most notable of which is *Ulrich's International Periodicals Directory*, which includes Canadian publications. Also, local community libraries often undertake the tedious process of indexing their home town papers.

Once you have pinpointed the journal, magazine, or newspaper you want, there is still the task of locating it. Several directories of libraries make it easier for you. There is the *Canadian Library Yearbook*, published by Micromedia Limited, and the *American Library Directory*, which, despite its title, has a Canadian section. It goes into a lot of detail, listing the number of volumes in a library and the library's book budget. The American directory gives the size of each library,

---

* *Author's note:* These sources are discussed in more depth in Chapter 12, "Using Libraries in Canada."

so the researcher has an idea of the likelihood of finding a publication or serial in a given library.

Here's another tip for locating publications in the public library system: look for "union lists." A union list has nothing to do with trade unions but is a directory of libraries that hold particular journals. For example, the public libraries in Toronto band together every two years to produce the *Guide to Periodicals and Newspapers in the Public Libraries of Metropolitan Toronto*. So if you were researching the pulp and paper industry in Canada, for instance, you could use this directory to learn what serialized publications cover that topic, in which libraries to find them, and how far back copies kept by those libraries go. There is also a massive union list issued by the National Library of Canada, called *Union List of Serials in the Social Sciences and Humanities Held by Canadian Libraries*. Also, the National Research Council publishes the *Union List of Scientific Serials in Canadian Libraries*.

Let's come back to a point I made earlier on local libraries. Don't think that small local libraries are inefficiently equipped to handle serious research projects. All libraries in Canada are linked together in formal or informal networks. If you went into a library in a small town, and its resources were not sufficient, that library could borrow the necessary material for you from a larger city library through an interlibrary loan. So there's a sort of ripple effect at work, from the small to medium to large libraries; small libraries are not shut out of the network.

Also, keep in mind that when you're doing research involving a small town or region, the local library has a lot of geographical, historical, and political material in various forms that might not be readily available in larger libraries (although you can, of course, arrange an interlibrary loan from a larger library).

Sometimes "special libraries" can be of assistance. These are libraries outside the public library system, to which the public can often gain access for serious research purposes when the sources are not available in the public library system. For example, let us say that you are researching an aspect of forestry and require a specialized journal that isn't available in the public library. The special forestry library at a university will probably keep that journal.

There are directories of special libraries for various regions in Canada. You can locate the associations that represent special libraries and publish these directories by checking the *Directory of Associations in Canada*. These associations sell their directories, although most public libraries have them on file.

Some special libraries have very small physical book collections; they usually have periodicals and reports, but their main tools are the telephone and computer terminal. Rather than operating a library in the traditional sense, special libraries often use a computer to identify what documents are available and then, by telephone, locate where the documents are. There are networks of special librarians, particularly where there is a subject affinity. They are in competition with each other, but they share the professional understanding that they assist each other to locate and lend materials and to advise on how to access information.

Another timesaver is to talk with a librarian who specializes in a particular area. You can often glean an enormous amount of information this way before you even start on a research project.

If you can't locate the information you need in a public or special library, ask the head librarian of a department for the name of an expert in the area you're researching. Head librarians can be extremely valuable sources for locating unusual experts. You can also refer, once again, to the *Directory of Associations in Canada*, which lists hundreds of organizations from coast to coast. They can either help you themselves or direct you to the appropriate source.

Research in the Sciences

*In the international scientific community, Dr. Louis Simino-
vitch is a well-known figure. He is the Director of Research at
Mount Sinai Hospital Research Institute in Toronto, former
President of the National Cancer Institute, and a professor in
and former Chairman of the Department of Medical Genetics at
the University of Toronto.*

*Dr. Siminovitch holds 18 prestigious honours and awards, in-
cluding that of Companion of the Order of Canada, the highest
civilian award in Canada. The author of 179 major scientific
articles and papers, he is currently on the editorial board of 10
medical journals.*

*Although research in the sciences is in many ways different
from gathering information in the humanities, there are a
number of overlapping techniques. In this interview, Dr.
Siminovitch reveals that the simple use of a network of information, such as telephone consultations with colleagues, can
yield information that has a profound effect on the medical
world. Literature searches, familiar to us in other contexts, also
play a significant role.*

Research in the sciences starts with an idea, something that
you're interested in. Your idea is based on your knowledge of

the existing literature. You know what the state of the art is, and you ask yourself: "What is the next important question that I have to address?" "Do I have the capacity to address this question?"

If you don't have the expertise, you must ask yourself whether or not you can acquire the knowledge easily. You don't want to formulate a trivial question, but rather one that is as important as possible. But you're always torn between the risky project and the one that is most likely to produce answers. This is because in order to be funded in science, you have to be able to show that you've produced something over a period of two to three years. These are the thought processes you go through. So, sometimes you don't end up where you started.

There are two kinds of science. One is observational science, where you look at things. The other is where you say to yourself: "I have an idea that this is the way that this particular thing works. I'm going to see if I can show that that is in fact the way it works." This is what I call "Cartesian reasoning." You're really going from A to B to C, in a very logical progression, and asking questions all the time. This second kind of science is what I practise. Also, I'm always asking a fairly well-defined question.

You're best off if you're in close contact with experts—to use the cliché, "in the network." A lot of information, some of it unpublished, surfaces at meetings. So your personality is important, because you have to be able to communicate easily with people.

Research in the sciences differs greatly from that in other disciplines. What scientists do in their work is to uncover what is already there—nature or, if you will, the absolute truth. In the humanities, researchers are creating and/or interpreting data as they see fit.

The starting point in the sciences, especially if you know little about a given field, is to do a systematic literature search. Today this can be done by computer, although many scientific publications are not yet indexed or abstracted on computer files. You should not only read the articles but also look at footnotes and bibliographies and follow up on them.

I get a lot of my information over the telephone. Telephone bills for scientists have gone up astronomically lately. I may be talking with a colleague, and she may tell me about someone who has just researched a new clone or come up with a new development in cancer research. Sometimes I just tell a colleague over the phone that I'm researching a particular problem and ask if he knows of anyone doing similar work.

My daughter, for instance, wanted to start researching a scientific project, but no articles had been published on the topic. She wanted to find out as much about this area as possible before she began her research, so she telephoned four scientists to find out if anyone in the network had done anything on the topic. Scientists work within a community, and each of us recognizes who the expert is in an area. This is especially true in larger cities. In Boston, for example, the details of an experiment are known within two days after it has begun, because there are so many scientists in the network, and everyone keeps up-to-date.

Another valuable source for me comes from applications for grants. Scientists sometimes ask me to referee their project, and they provide me with all the published articles and reports on that topic.

And, believe it or not, scientists sometimes obtain information from reading newspapers. I recently read in the newspaper about research that is being conducted in England into a cancer gene—four weeks before the medical journals picked it up!

A Lawyer's Methods

*When it comes to libel and slander law, many Canadian maga-
zines and newspapers choose to consult with lawyer Julian
Porter. In 20 years of practice, Porter has established himself as
one of the most capable—and controversial—lawyers in the
country. One might think that this Queen's Counsel's methods
of research are sophisticated and difficult to master. But Porter,
like many of the other specialists in this book, actually uses
down-to-earth approaches to assembling information. He prefers to observe things first-hand, interview his clients directly,
read original documents himself, and consult with experts to
see if he's on the right track. It's a formula that evidently works
well for him. Here he recounts a few of his more memorable
cases.*

Facts, and how you present them, determine the outcome of
a lawsuit. I prefer to use the old-fashioned way of gathering
facts. I talk to a witness myself, before he or she testifies. A
junior lawyer might not follow up on the little avenues in a conversation that can lead to a goldmine of information. Someone
who is less experienced than me might not recognize the significance of what otherwise might be just a tiny little fact.

You really have to do primary research to establish the facts. All lawyers say that the facts are already there, but the truth of the matter is that the facts are how you arrange them. Keep in mind that a jury trial is a moving opera. There is a series of facts on a piece of paper, and there are five different lawyers presenting these facts with five totally different impressions. It all comes down to how you've conducted your initial interviews and assembled your information. In court, part of your job is to stay away from asking questions that can hurt your client.

When I interview my client before the trial takes place, I always ask, "Is there anything else that I've left out?" Or: "Anything I should ask?" Or: "Anything you want to ask me?" Open-ended questions like these are often very important and yield interesting information. I take a brutal approach with my client, much worse than an interrogation. This is the only way to prepare the person for the trial. On the other hand, when I interview a witness before a trial takes place, I usually take a soft approach.

I learned an important lesson in research when I was acting as an assistant crown prosecutor in a large tax evasion case, a case that became known as "The Great Sweet Grass Scandal." The case involved a series of interlocking companies whose shares were shuffled around and sold at inflated prices. The guilty party pretended the profits were going to outside purchasers, but he was eventually charged and convicted of tax evasion.

In this case Walter Williston, the senior prosecutor, taught me to personally examine all documents in the *original*—not the photocopies—because you miss any markings that may be on the backs of the originals. There were about 100,000 pieces of paper involved in this case, and I looked at all of them over a one-and-a-half-year period, then drew my conclusions. I could sense that the minutes had been redone. Some of the minutes and daily deposit books had been typed on a machine that had a broken letter "t." Typewriter experts studied the documents, and we were able to prove that two typewriters had been used. It took a lot of time to sort out, but this was a scam, meant to confuse anyone looking into it.

Young lawyers frantically read the law in their field. When you get older, however, you rely more on your own judgement. I now understand the basis of the law and usually ask a junior to look up existing cases for me. This can be done by using various indexes. I read and reread the cases to prepare myself. It pays to work with another person on the research, because that person may have a different point of view on a matter. He or she may well be right, and I may be wrong.

Sometimes a computer can help you do research. I once acted for Canadian artist Michael Snow, who was suing Eaton's because the company had attached red ribbons to his sculptured geese (which hang in downtown Toronto's Eaton Centre) as part of their Christmas decorations. This was an infringement of Section 14 of the Copyright Act. There weren't any reported decisions on this section. My junior, however, did a computer search at the Osgoode Hall law library and turned up one unreported case. I also learned of a lawyer who had written a paper on that section of the act, and in that paper there was mention of another unreported case. To round off our research, we looked through European law books to find cases that discussed how the issue was dealt with outside Canada.

It can help to do some research on the judge and the opposing lawyer. This information can help me decide how to present my case. It's important to know in advance who the judge is going to be. I try to ascertain what he or she knows about the law in my field. If, for instance, the judge is an expert on libel and slander, when I stand up in court I get right to the point immediately, stating what the issues are. But if the judge isn't well versed in that area of law, I first set out the principles and try to persuade the judge in a more subtle way. There are books available on the background of judges, but at this point in my career I usually know most of their backgrounds.

The same is true of lawyers, and if I'm unfamiliar with a lawyer I quickly try to learn if the person is clever. I'm not saying that *I'm* all that smart, but it makes a considerable difference if you're organizing a case with a lawyer who is either not as bright as you or a lot brighter than you. In court you throw out information, assuming that the other lawyer is taking it and running with it in a certain way. If the two of you are not on the same wave length, one of you is going to miss the boat.

I can tell a lot about the other lawyer just by the statement of claim he files, outlining his defence. This tells me right away if he knows his law or not. I also learn something if there is trouble setting a date for the legal proceedings. If the other lawyer is too busy or blames her secretary, this tells me something about her competence.

During the actual examination for discovery, when both sides present arguments for taking the matter before a court, I usually look at the way the lawyer organizes his papers. If they're scattered across the desk in a sloppy fashion, this may indicate he is confused. Thus, personal observations can be useful. Finally, if it's necessary to supplement this information, I may ask colleagues about the lawyer.

By the time the trial takes place, I can tell if I can get away with a few things during cross-examination. I may realize that the other lawyer doesn't have all the necessary papers at her fingertips, so I may be able to make statements that she can't dispute without a copy of the paper I have in front of me. Also, I may be able to pose a few leading questions to my witness without the other lawyer catching on. All of this may be possible with a sloppy lawyer, but not with a tough, highly efficient counsel.

In addition to these straightforward methods of research, I might also pick up the telephone and consult with a leading expert in a field. I am never embarrassed to ask for advice. This advice tells me if my judgement is correct. If I get the feeling that I'm on the right track, I then follow it up by using other resources.

SOURCES

PART TWO

Using Libraries in Canada

There are at least three things you can be sure of about libraries: they collect information on *every* subject; the information can *always* be located; and the library personnel (which, in this chapter, refers to librarians, library technicians, and other information specialists) who run them have been educated to meet your information needs.

Surprisingly, libraries are often overlooked as a source of information. This is an irony of monumental proportion, because they are in fact the best source of all. There are thousands of highly skilled library professionals across Canada willing to assist anyone involved in research—very often free of charge—and millions of books, periodicals, specialized collections, and computer services at your fingertips. The only prerequisite for using a library successfully is the ability to ask questions.

There are four types of libraries in Canada: public, academic (on college and university campuses), school, and special libraries (which meet the internal needs of government departments, businesses, and institutions).

Public libraries are tax-supported and accessible to the public. The policies of academic and school libraries vary, but access can generally be obtained by legitimate researchers. Special libraries, generally speaking, are privately supported and not always open to the public, although special arrangements can sometimes be made. Let's examine each type of library in greater detail.

PUBLIC LIBRARIES

There are over 3,000 public libraries scattered from coast to coast. Public libraries are governed by provincial laws and regulations and are designed to meet the information needs of local communities. As a resident of a community, you can borrow library materials once you have registered with your nearest library; most libraries issue identification cards that allow the holders to borrow library materials. If you want only to use the facilities, there is no registration requirement, although you should introduce yourself at the reference desk out of politeness.

Dealing with Library Personnel   Research is very much a social skill, and this is especially evident in a library. You have a right to any information in a public library, but you may walk away empty-handed if you have not behaved toward the staff in a socially acceptable fashion. If you find yourself having to line up at an information desk, be patient—it's usually well worth the wait. With library budget cutbacks, it may be that you have to wait longer than on previous visits. Still, avoid wording your request in a negative way or pointing out to the staff that you're unhappy about having to wait.

Just as important is how you *word* your request. It is important to give as much specific information as possible and to put your question in context. Only then can the staff assist you in the fullest possible way. For example, if you are writing a business report and require the Canadian dollar value of nickel exports, you should ask for that, not for something as vague as "trade statistics."

Finally, if your research needs are serious, make sure the library staff know it. The library personnel usually points out basic sources for everyday, casual information requests. They will spend more time and point out sophisticated sources once they realize that your information request is a more complex one. If they cannot help you, request an interview with the department expert on the subject area you are researching.

Vertical Files   An easy way to find information is to use the material in a library's vertical file. A business magazine once asked me to write profiles of thirteen Canadian business leaders. I was given only two weeks to complete the job, which left me very little time for the research. I knew almost nothing about the people I was to interview, but fortunately, the Metropolitan Toronto Library came to my rescue. The person at the information desk told me that the reference library used two filing cabinets to store newspaper and magazine clippings on notable Canadians. Using these files, I was able to acquire a quick overview of the business leaders and formulate specific interview questions.

Each library, of course, has its own filing system, and the quality of the material varies considerably from library to library. Larger libraries, which are divided into different subject departments, may or may not use filing cabinets to file material. Inquire at the information desk of each department to find out if such files exist.

Finding Books Quickly   Never walk into a library expecting all of its holdings to be listed in one catalogue. Every library has its own way of cataloguing its book collection. There was a time when you could safely assume that all libraries kept a card catalogue to list their books, but with changing technology there are now at least two other popular methods of doing this: various microforms (microfilm and microfiche) and on-line computer services. Most of the smaller libraries still prefer to use card catalogues, but more and more of the larger libraries are switching to other space- and cost-saving methods; some libraries use a combination of card catalogue and other methods. The quickest way to sort out this confusion is to ask at the reference desk how the library lists its holdings.

Now you know where to search for books. You can search for the author, title, or subject. Library book catalogues use various combinations of these, all of which are in alphabetical order. However, the alphabetical order may, at times, be quite complicated. Don't hesitate to ask the library staff for an explanation. It is very common to find the author and title in one catalogue and the subject listings in another.

You may find it difficult at times to identify an author. There isn't any confusion with an author who uses a personal name, like Stephen Overbury, but if the author is a *corporate body*, it becomes a little harder. (Corporate bodies may include associations, institutions, business firms, non-profit enterprises, governments, government agencies, religious bodies, local churches and conferences.) For example, if the author were the "Ministry of Citizenship," it wouldn't necessarily follow that the author would be catalogued that way. It may be that you would look under "Ontario Government. Ministry of Citizenship." Cataloguing can thus become confusing, so it's a good idea to ask at the reference desk for assistance.

Once you locate the correct title and author of a book, you have to determine where in the library the book is kept. This is more important in smaller- to medium-sized libraries, where you find open stacks and select the material yourself. Larger libraries, however, often have closed stacks, which means you will fill out a book request slip, using the call number from the catalogue, hand the slip in at the information desk, and wait for the library staff to bring you the book.

Libraries usually use either the Dewey Decimal System (which you can recognize by initial numbers from zero to nine) or the Library of Congress System (which contains letters, followed by numbers, unless you're looking in a medical library). Books catalogued under these systems are shelved by subject, permitting users both to browse and locate a particular book.

Serials   Newspapers, magazines, and journals (which librarians call serials because they are issued in series) are often catalogued separately from the main library catalogue. The same is generally true of government publications. Again, it is useful to ask the reference staff where these are shelved and where you can find an index to use them more efficiently.

Interlibrary Loans   If your local library doesn't have a copy of a book or other material you seek, it may be possible to get it through an interlibrary loan. The beauty of Canada's library system is that virtually all libraries, regardless of their size, are linked with each other through formal or informal networks, as Brian Land pointed out in Chapter 9.

If neither you nor the library personnel can trace a book, ask that they contact the National Library of Canada in Ottawa. This library has a massive card catalogue ("union" catalogue) listing 13 million books in the social sciences and humanities that are available in 300 Canadian libraries. This card catalogue listing ended in 1980; later entries are kept on a computer listing. (Similar union listings of social science and science periodicals are kept at the Canada Institute for Scientific and Technical Information or CISTI. CISTI is, in effect, the National Science Library.)

The National Library prefers requests to come from a librarian, but will answer questions directly from the public. With its cataloguing system it can often tell you which libraries keep the books you're looking for. You can then arrange an inter-library loan through your local library. If you want to locate a Canadian book, the National Library is an excellent source, because part of its mandate is to keep a copy of every book published in Canada. So, it can also provide you with information on Canadian subjects, in answer to specific questions, if your local library is unable to help.

The National Library also maintains contact with libraries around the world. Its collection includes union catalogues from other countries and on-line access to shared cataloguing databases, and can, therefore, conduct international searches to locate needed items upon request.

Reference Books   All libraries keep a wide selection of reference books and considerable information can be found examining the right one. Indeed, books have been written on the value of reference books. The comments made here should be taken as an introduction to the topic, nothing more.

To get an idea of the tremendous variety of Canadian reference books, refer to an excellent library science text by Dorothy Ryder, *Canadian Reference Sources*, published by the Canadian Library Association in 1981. Its information is brought up-to-date in an informative article by Edith T. Jarvi and Diane Henderson, "Canadian Reference Books; Or Benevolent Ignorance Dispelled," in a 1983 issue of *Reference Services Review*.

Another useful aid is the *Guide to Basic Reference Materials for Canadian Libraries*, edited by Claire England and others and published periodically by the University of Toronto Press.

Because of the variety of reference books available, using them can save a lot of time. For example, I once required some information quickly on a Nazi war criminal and found that the history department of my local library had a copy of *Who Was Who in Nazi Germany* by Robert Wistrich. This work answered my questions.

On another occasion, when a friend asked me for information on raising dogs in Canada, the *Directory of Associations in*

Canada was very helpful. Figure 12.1 shows a page from the "Subject Index" of the directory. Under the heading "Dogs" are eight references to dog associations, one of which turned out to have all the information I needed. The address of the Canadian Kennel Club appears in the third column in Figure 12.2 in the "Alphabetical List of Associations." This directory is really very simple to use.

Whenever I need quick information on Canadian companies, I begin by referring to reference books written or edited by Brian Land, but you can be assured that whatever your subject, there is probably a handy reference book on it.

Periodical Indexes   If you want to locate an article in a newspaper, magazine, journal, or report, you should familiarize yourself with periodical indexes. These may appear intimidating because of their size, small print, and numerous abbreviations. With a little practice, however, you will find that indexes are not complicated to use and can save you the tedious job of skimming through countless back issues of periodicals. Canada has at least four key indexes you should be aware of.

The *Canadian News Index (CNI)*, published by Micromedia Limited, Toronto, indexes seven of the country's major daily newspapers: the *Calgary Herald*, the *Toronto Star*, the *Globe and Mail*, the *Vancouver Sun*, the *Winnipeg Free Press*, the *Montreal Gazette*, and the *Halifax Chronicle Herald*.

CNI is published monthly in a magazine format and republished in one volume at the end of each year. The key to its abbreviations is located at the bottom of every page. It is separated into two sections: the subject index and the personal name index. If, for example, you want to know which articles have been written on the asbestos industry in Quebec, you would look under the subject heading, "Asbestos Industry," and then under the sub-heading, "Quebec (Province)." As shown in Figure 12.3, an article from the *Montreal Gazette*, dated January 10, 1987 and on page B1, will be found under this sub-heading.

If you are researching an individual, you would look in the Personal Name Index section. For example, if you were interested in any articles on singer Anne Murray, you would find a variety of them listed under her name (as Figure 12.4 shows).

Micromedia also publishes the *Canadian Business Index (CBI)*, which indexes about 200 leading Canadian business magazines. Like the *CNI*, it is published monthly and cumulated as a single-volume index at the end of the year. Three distinct sections of the *CBI* enable a researcher to search for articles by subject, corporate name, and personal name or cross-reference all three. For example, as you can see in Figure 12.5, you could research cars by looking under the subject heading, "Automobiles," the corporate name, "General Motors," or the personal name of the company's chairman, "Roger Smith."

You can use the *Microlog Index* to search for municipal, provincial, and federal government publications, as well as privately published materials from non-government research institutions, professional associations, and special interest groups. The index, also published by Micromedia, is divided into a main section (which lists all materials by individual and corporate authors), subject section, and title section.

One of Canada's oldest indexes is the *Canadian Periodical Index (CPI)*, formerly compiled by the Canadian Library Association but, since 1987, owned by Info Globe, a division of the *Globe and Mail*. Its publication dates back to at least 1928 and indexes approximately 350 French and English periodicals, many of which are not included in the indexes mentioned above.

Canadian Magazine Index, published by Micromedia Limited, indexes approximately 300 Canadian magazines.

Many other publications, particularly those which are non-Canadian, are not included in these indexes. Some publications, such as the *New York Times* and the *Times* of London, publish their own indexes. To find out if the publication you seek has a separate index and/or is indexed in a central source, refer to *Ulrich's International Periodicals Directory* or the *Standard Periodical Directory*.

Statistics   An important new source of statistical data is the *Canadian Statistical Index (CSI)*, published by Micromedia Limited. Published as a clothbound annual early each year, it is supplemented by a paperback issue which appears each fall. The *CSI* indexes statistics appearing in both governmental and non-governmental sources.

Computer Services   Indexes, along with scores of other valuable information sources, are becoming increasingly available through computer searches. Furthermore, you don't need to own a computer to take advantage of their obvious time-saving abilities. This is because many of Canada's larger public libraries now maintain a computer search centre.

Figure 12.1   From the *Directory of Associations in Canada*

Disabled

Skills Training and Support Services Association
Société pour les enfants handicapés du Québec
The Society for Housing of Physically Handicapped Young Adults
Society for Knowledge in Learning Living Skills of Greater Edmonton
Society for Manitobans with Disabilities Inc.
Southern Alberta Community Living Association
Southwestern Organization for the Rights of the Disabled
Step-By-Step Preschool Society
Thunder Bay Equestrian Association for the Disabled
United Handicapped Groups of Ontario
Valleyview and District Association for the Handicapped
Variety Club of Ontario, Tent #28
The War Amputations of Canada (Canadian Amputees Foundation)
Windsor Association Riding for the Handicapped
Workshop Council of Nova Scotia
Yukon Rehabilitation Centre Society
Yukon Special Olympics

Disarmament *See* **Arms control**

Diseases
See also Names of specific diseases
Canadian Infectious Disease Society
Community and Hospital Infection Control Association - Canada
Kildonan Foundation Society
Queen Elizabeth II Canadian Fund to Aid in Research on the Diseases of Children
Society for Mucopolysaccharide Diseases

Disques *Voir* **Records and recording**

Distilleries *Voir* **Liquor**

Distilling *See* **Liquor**

Distributeurs automatiques *Voir* **Vending machines**

Distributeurs d'automobiles *Voir* **Automobile dealers**

Distribution
Pacific Brewers' Distributors Ltd.

Distribution (commerce) *Voir* **Marketing**

Distrophic epidermolysis bullosa
Distrophic Epidermolysis Bullosa Research Association

Diving
See also Scuba diving; Skin diving
British Columbia Summer Swimming Association
Canadian Amateur Diving Association, Inc.
Canadian Association of Diving Contractors
Fédération du plongeon amateur du Québec
New Brunswick Underwater Council
Newfoundland Diving Association
Northwest Territories Underwater Council
Nova Scotia Amateur Diving Association
Saskatchewan Amateur Diving Association
Saskatchewan Underwater Council, Inc.

Yukon Underwater Divers Association

Dockers *Voir* **Stevedores**

Doctors *See* **Physicians**

Documents officiels, Organisation de *Voir* **Records management**

Dogs
Canadian Association of Guide Dog Users Inc.
Canadian Greyhound Racing and Breeders Association
Canadian Kennel Club
Edmonton Springer Spaniel Club
The National Retriever Club of Canada
Ontario Greyhound Breeders Association Inc.
Ottawa Valley Gun Dog Club
Western Federation of Individuals and Dog Organizations

Domestics
International Coalition To End Domestic Workers Exploitation

Domestiques *Voir* **Domestics**

Dons *Voir* **Charitable contributions**

Doors *See* **Building materials and supplies**

Dossiers médicaux *Voir* **Medical records**

Down *See* **Feathers**

Drama *See* **Theatre**

Driver education
Canadian Professional Driver Education Association

Droit *Voir* **Law**

Droit d'auteur *Voir* **Copyright**

Droit de propriété *Voir* **Real estate**

Droit de publication *Voir* **Copyright**

Droit de réproduction *Voir* **Copyright**

Droits civiques *Voir* **Civil liberties**

Drug abuse
See also Alcohol and alcoholism
Alcohol and Drug Concerns, Inc.
Alcohol and Drug Dependency Commission of Newfoundland and Labrador
Alcohol and Drug Dependency Information and Counselling Services
Alcoholism and Drug Addiction Research Foundation
The Alcoholism Foundation of Manitoba
Canadian Addictions Foundation
Connection Drug Rehabilitation Society
Council on Drug Abuse
Crossroads Treatment Centre Society
Drug Education Co-ordinating Council
Interior Native Alcohol and Drug Abuse Society
Kamloops Society for Alcohol and Drug Services
Moose Jaw Alcohol and Drug Abuse Society Inc.

Economic and industrial development

Nechi Institute on Drug and Alcohol Education
Parent Resources Institute for Drug Education
Parents Against Drugs

Drug industry
See also Pharmacy
L'Association des fabricants du Québec des produits pharmaceutiques
Canadian Association of Pharmacy Technicians
Canadian Drug Manufacturers Association
Canadian Society of Industrial Pharmacists
Canadian Wholesale Drug Association
Council for the Accreditation of Pharmaceutical Manufacturers Representatives of Canada
Nonprescription Drug Manufacturers Association of Canada
Pharmaceutical Advertising Advisory Board
The Pharmaceutical and Toilet Preparations Traffic Association
Pharmaceutical Manufacturers Association of Canada

Drugs *See* **Drug abuse; Drug industry**

Drunk drivers *See* **Impaired driving**

Drywall construction *See* **Construction**

Dutch *See* **Netherlands and the Dutch**

Dystonia
Dystonia Medical Research Foundation

Dystonie *Voir* **Dystonia**

Dystrophie musculaire *Voir* **Muscular Dystrophy**

Ear
British Columbia Ear Bank

Earth sciences *See* **Geology**

East Timor
Nova Scotia East Timor Group

Eau *Voir* **Water and water works**

Eau, Pollution de l' *Voir* **Pollution**

Eaus d'égouts *Voir* **Sanitation and sewer construction**

Ebénisterie *Voir* **Woodworking**

Echanges d'étudiants *Voir* **Educational exchanges**

Echecs *Voir* **Chess**

Eclairage *Voir* **Lighting**

Ecoles *Voir* **Schools**

Ecoles communautaires *Voir* **Community schools**

Ecologie *Voir* **Conservation and the environment**

Ecology *See* **Conservation and the environment**

Economic and industrial development
See also Single industry communities
ASEAN-Canada Business Council
Atlantic Provinces Economic Council

Figure 12.2 From the *Directory of Associations in Canada*

Canadian Intramural Recreation Association

Corporate members: 130
Pub: CIRA Bulletin, 8 p.a.
○1988: May 26–29, Halifax, N.S.

The Canadian Intravenous Nurses Association Inc./Association canadienne des infirmières(iers) en soins intraveineux (1975)
4433 Sheppard Ave. East, Suite 200, Agincourt, Ont. M1S 1V3
Tel: (416) 292-0687
Office Mgr: Pamela Smith
Employees: 1 *Individual members:* 400
Pub: C.I.N.A. Journal, q.
○1988: Oct. 20–21, Scarborough, Ont.
Also called/Aussi connu par: CINA

Canadian Islamic Cultural and Educational Foundation
13070 - 113th St., Edmonton, Alta. T5E 5A8 *Tel:* (403) 451-6695
Pres: Pelil Rahime

Canadian-Italian Business and Professional Association
See/Voir L'Association des gens d'affaires et professionnels Italo-Canadiens Inc.

Canadian Italian Business and Professional Association of Toronto/ L'Association des hommes d'affaires et professionnels canadiens-italiens (1952)
901 Lawrence Ave. West, Suite 212, Toronto, Ont. M6A 1C3 *Tel:* (416) 782-4445
Employees: 2 *Individual members:* 440
Pub: Directory, a.

Canadian Italian Historical Association
252 Bloor St. West Suite S826, Toronto, Ont. M5S 1V5

Canadian Jersey Cattle Club/Cercle canadien des bovins jerseys (1901)
343 Waterloo Ave., Guelph, Ont. N1H 3K1
Tel: (519) 821-1020
Sec: Russell G. Gammon
Employees: 5 + 1 p.t. *Individual members:* 820
Pub: Canadian Jersey Breeder, 11 p.a.
○1988: April 2, Brandon, Man.
Also called/Aussi connu par: Jersey Canada
●*Member of* Dairy Farmers of Canada: see listing

Canadian Jesuit Missions (1947)
1190 Danforth Ave., Toronto, Ont. M4J 1M6 *Tel:* (416) 465-1824
Dir: Robert Gaudet
Employees: 6 + 1 FTE + 1 volunteer
Pub: Canadian Jesuit Missions, 5 p.a.; *Canadian Jesuit Missions Calendar,* a.
○1988, 1989, 1990: Dec. 31, Toronto, Ont.

Canadian Jesuit Refugee Program*
Jesuit Centre, 947 Queen St. East, Toronto, Ont. M4M 1J9 *Tel:* (416) 469-1123
Educator: Colin MacAdam

Canadian Jewellers Association/ Association canadienne des bijoutiers (1918)
20 Eglinton Ave. West, Suite 1203, Toronto, Ont. M4R 1K8 *Tel:* (416) 480-1424
Gen. Mgr: John Theo
Employees: 10 *Corporate members:* 1700
Pub: Jewellery World Magazine, 6 p.a.; *JW Plus*
○1988: June 5–8, Ont.; 1989: June 4–7, St. John's Nfld.; 1990: May 12–15, Vancouver, B.C.

Canadian Jewellers Institute
20 Eglinton Ave. West, Suite 1203, Toronto, Ont. M4R 1K8 *Tel:* (416) 480-1424
Gen. Mgr: John Theo
Pub: Newsviews, q.

Canadian Jewellery Group Co-operative Association
239 Pembroke St. West, Pembroke, Ont. K8A 5N4 *Tel:* (613) 735-4145

Canadian Jewellery Travellers Association
1491 Yonge St., Toronto, Ont. M4T 1Z4
Tel: (416) 922-9901

Canadian Jewish Congress/Congrès juif canadien (1919)
1590 Docteur Penfield Ave., Montreal, Que. H3G 1C5 *Tel:* (514) 931-7531
Nat. Exec. Dir: M. Jack Silverstone
●*Member of* Canadian Ethnocultural Council; see listing
- Calgary Region
1607 - 90th Ave. S.W., Calgary, Alta. T2V 4V7 *Tel:* (403) 253-8600
Exec. Dir: Drew Staffenberg
Also called: Calgary Jewish Community Council
- Manitoba Region
370 Hargrave St., Winnipeg, Man. R3B 2K1
Tel: (204) 943-0406
Exec. Dir: Robert Freedman
- Maritime Region
1515 South Park St., Suite 304, Halifax, N.S. B3J 2L2
Exec. Dir: Shimon Fogel
- Ontario Region (1919)
4600 Bathurst St., Willowdale, Ont. M2R 3V2 *Tel:* (416) 635-2883
Exec. Dir: Dr. Edmond Y. Lipsitz
Employees: 11 + 2 p.t.
- Pacific Region
950 West 41st Ave., Vancouver, B.C. V5Z 2N7 *Tel:* (604) 261-8101
Exec. Dir: Erwin Nest
- Quebec Region
1590 Docteur Penfield Ave., Montreal, Que. H3G 1C5 *Tel:* (514) 931-7531
Exec. Dir: Jeff D. Kushner

Canadian Jewish Historical Society
2525 Mark Ave., Windsor, Ont. N9E 2W2
Tel: (519) 969-2422
Rep: Jonathon V. Plaut

Canadian Jiu-jitsu Association/ Association canadienne de jiu-jitsu (1963)
Pres: R.W. Forrester
1309 Falgarwood Dr., Oakville.

Ont. L6H 2L7 *Tel:* (416) 844-8750
Employees: 10 volunteers
Individual members: 3000
○1988, 1989, 1990: April 1, Oakville, Ont.

Canadian Judicial Council/Conseil Canadien de la Magistrature (1971)
130 Albert St., Suite 717, Ottawa, Ont. K1A 0W8 *Tel:* (613) 998-5182
Exec. Sec: Jeannie Thomas
Employees: 3
○1988: Aug., Saint John, N.B.

Canadian Junior Ballet Society
15 Armour Blvd., Toronto, Ont. M5M 3B9
Tel: (416) 489-7597

Canadian Junior Chamber-Jaycees/ Jeune chambre du Canada-Jaycees (1923)
Exec. Dir: Luc Bégin
39 Leacock Way, Kanata, Ont. K2K 1T1
Tel: (613) 592-2450
Employees: 3 + 1 p.t. *Individual members:* 3000
Pub: Canadian Jaycee Canadien, q.; *National Directory*
Mailing lists available: Yes
○1988: July, Thunder Bay, Ont.; 1989: July, Barrie, Ont.

Canadian Juvenile Products Association (1986)
P.O. Box 294, Kleinburg, Ont. J0J 1C0
Tel: (416) 893-1689
Exec. Dir: Henry Wittenburg
Employees: 2 *Individual members:* 15

Canadian Karate Kung-Fu Association
702 Spadina Ave., Toronto, Ont. M5S 2J2
Tel: (416) 922-3850

Canadian Kendo Federation/Fédération canadienne de Kendo
Sec: S. Uyenaka
150 Lesmill Rd., Don Mills, Ont. M3B 2T5
Tel: (416) 445-7813

Canadian Kennel Club/Le Cercle canadien du chenil (1888)
2150 Bloor St. West, Toronto, Ont. M6S 4V7 *Tel:* (416) 763-4391
Sec.-Treas: John C. Gough
Employees: 65 *Individual members:* 14067

Canadian Kitchen Cabinet Association/ Association canadienne de fabricants d'armoires de cuisine (1969)
27 Goulburn Ave., Ottawa, Ont. K1N 8C7
Tel: (613) 233-6205 *Telex:* 053-4519
Exec. Vice-Pres: J.F. McCracken
Employees: 2 *Individual members:* 95
Corporate members: 55
●*Management services provided by* Canadian Lumberman's Association; see listing

Canadian Kodakan Black Belt Association/Association canadienne des ceintures noires du kodokan (1956)
333 River Rd., Tower C, 10th Floor, Vanier, Ont. K1L 8H9 *Tel:* (613) 748-5640
Telex: 053-3660
Exec. Dir: Donna White
Employees: 6 + 2 p.t. + 50+ volunteers
Individual members: 3000

Figure 12.3   From the *Canadian News Index*

SUBJECT INDEX   67

Arts festivals (cont'd)
Festival salutes sweep of Italy's culture
● *TS* O 2'87 pE3
"Matchmaker" brought together two countries
●(F) *SS* O 4'87 pD5
Festival goes high- and low-brow ◆ *G&M*
O 29'87 pD6
New York aims to capture spirit of 20th century
with arts festival MG D 12'87 pJ9
Olympic festival set to showcase Canadian talent
TS D 28'87 pC7

ArtsFund
ArtsFund: benefits for the fringe MG O 1'87
pE3
Helping artists cope financially ◆ *G&M* O 6'87
pD9

Artspace Inc.
Artspace forced to shell out before new tenant
moves in *WFP* Ag 14'87 p31

Asamera Inc.
Asamera to spend $36m in '87 *CH* My 16'87
pH2
Gold's volatility kills share issue *CH* Je 24'87
pE1

Asbestos
Asbestos closes hospital project *VS* F 12'87
pA13
Canada asks US agency to rethink asbestos
plan ◆ *MG* F 20'87 pB14
Ontario to investigate asbestos illness claims
G&M Mr 6'87 pA13
Asbestos in building sparks student protest *G&M*
Mr 13'87 pD12
York University to remove some asbestos from
law school *TS* Mr 25'87 pA30
Asbestos pitched abroad: MD pushes for
buyer-beware program *VS* My 4'87 pB2
Asbestos controversy heats up: can magic
mineral be tamed? # *TS* My 16'87
pA1.A10
Rehabilitating the lethal image of asbestos *G&M*
My 16'87 pD1.D2
Ceiling asbestos poses 'no hazard' at Halifax
airport *HCH* Je 2'87 p9
Rehab union wants study *HCH* Jl 21'87 p3
Asbestos is found, building evacuated MG
Jl 24'87 pA3
Local firm (American Environmental Enterprises
Corp) finds opportunity in asbestos problem *CH*
S 2'87 pF1
Third World struggle: Canada's promotion of
mineral is inviting disaster, officials say -
Asbestos and your health, part 3 (F) *WFP*
O 5'87 p13,14
The selling of asbestos: Canada eyes the Third
World ●(F) MG O 22'87 pA1,A2

Carcinogenic effects
Dying man fights for compensation *VS* Ja 26'87,
pA1,A2
Cancer victim (John Kingsbury) fights for funds
◆ *CH* Ja 27'87 pA7
WCB puts rush on review in case of dying
miner *VS* Ja 27'87 pA9
Deadly cover-up alleged *WFP* F 26'87 p7
Second-hand exposure: asbestos and your
health, part 1 (F) *WFP* O 3'87 p49,50
Asbestos and your health: because law different,
Canadians seldom sue *WFP* O 6'87 p29
Asbestos and your health: danger lurks
everywhere ●(F) *WFP* O 6'87 p27

Laws and regulations
(Manitoba) NDP attacked on asbestos support
WFP D 2'86 p6
Proposed asbestos ban 'draconian, unjustified' -
Nash and Houston *TS* Mr 12'87 pA19
Asbestos issue seen as comparable to acid rain
- Silbergeld and Percival *TS* Mr 13'87 pA17
Industry calls for worldwide controls on asbestos
MG My 22'87 pB5
Asbestos removal work "couldn't get any
worse" (F) *CH* Je 8'87 pB1

Substitutes
Asbestos substitutes dangerous, Masse says
◆ *TS* Mr 30'87 pD10
Asbestos substitutes may pose health risk
●(F) *CH* My 4'87 pC2

Asbestos Corp. Ltd.
Asbestos minority holders sek follow-up bid
G&M N 19'87 pB6
Asbestos shareholders fight for followup offer
◆ *MG* N 19'87 pC1
Dispute renewed ◆ *WFP* N 19'87 p55

Asbestos industry

Safety measures
Foreign asbestos safety pushed *CH* My 1'87
pB8

Newfoundland
Newfoundland to complete purchase of $12m
Baie Verte Mines shares *G&M* Jl 11'87 pB5
Nfld aids Baie Verte mine ◆ *HCH* D 26'87
p38

Quebec (Province)
Asbestos: Quebec dream turns to dust
●(F) MG Ja 10'87 pB1
Good money after bad? MG Je 19'87 pB2

Asbestos International Association
Industry calls for worldwide controls on asbestos
MG My 22'87 pB5

Ascorbic acid *See* Vitamins and minerals

ASEA Inc.
ASEA wins $315m contract for Hydro-Quebec
substations MG F 4'87 pF1

Ash
See also Coal

Asia
See also Southeast Asia
South Asia's certainty: poverty and
unemployment *SS* Ja 4'87 pH1,H4
Sun sets on love Asian leaders ● *TS*
Jl 5'87 pH5
Freak weather triggers food crisis in Asia *TS*
S 3'87 pA16
Asia's trading 'dragons' fear US recession *CH*
N 1'87 pC5
Ferry disasters plague poor Asian countries *CH*
D 23'87 pA5

Asia Pacific Region
Asia Pacific report (F) *G&M* S 18'87 pC1,C2-

Asian Canadians
See also Chinese Canadians: Filipino
Canadians: Japanese Canadians: Sri Lankan
Canadians: Vietnamese Canadians
Vancouver police fear Asian gang war ◆ *WFP*
Ja 25'87 p1
Determined Asians go to top of the class
●(F) *MG* Ja 27'87 pA1,A6
Cooperation seen as key to ending gang
violence *VS* Ja 29'87 pA9
Yee urges meeting to halt youth gangs *VS*
Ja 30'87 pA13
Premier offers help in fight against Asian gangs
◆ *CH* Ja 30'87 pA13
BC Asian groups need more money, Sihota
says ◆ *VS* Je 25'87 pB2
Youth with gang links found slain ◆
VS S 19'87 pA1,A2
Police fear gangs widening net concerns over
recruitment raised after teenager found slain in
home *VS* S 22'87 pA3
AG declares war on gang violence *VS* O 8'87
pA1,A2
Gang squad appeals for help in battle *VS*
O 9'87 pB1,B8

Asparagus
Asparagus: tender is the white ● *MG*
My 6'87 pE1
Asparagus a delicious harbinger of spring *TS*
My 20'87 pC1

Aspartame
Manufacturer keen to squash fears about safety
of aspartame *VS* Ja 21'87 pC5
New studies question safety of aspartame *TS*
Je 8'87 pC1,C2
Some scientists souring on aspartame's safety
(F) *CH* Je 15'87 pB4
NutraSweet's grip on aspartame puts pop firms
in a fizz *TS* Je 23'87 pC1
Patent on sweetener is extended after Quebec
ruling gets factory *G&M* Je 23'87 pA1,A2

Aspartame (cont'd)
Bill lengthening patent on sweetener aspartame
likely to get public airing *G&M* Je 24'87 pB11
FDA's approval of aspartame under scrutiny
G&M Je 24'87 pB21
NutraSweet monopoly to be costly, group says
TS Je 24'87 pE3
Sweetener patent extension could cost us
$100m ◆ *VS* Je 24'87 pA7
Consumers called losers in patent case *G&M*
Je 25'87 pB1
Aspartame patent foes win round ◆ *CH*
Je 26'87 pB5
Senate slows down NutraSweet patent bill *G&M*
Je 27'87 pB4
Senators sour attempt to extend patent 5 years
◆ *MG* Je 27'87 pA9
Sweetener monopoly extension cut short by
Senate changes *TS* Ja 27'87 pA11
Firm to lose sweetener patent but soda prices
unlikely to drop *TS* Jl 1'87 pA3
NutraSweet is denied extension of patent *G&M*
Jl 1'87 pA5
Bill to extend patent on NutraSweet fails ◆
MG Jl 2'87 pB1
New fears surface concerning aspartame *G&M*
Jl 7'87 pA10
NutraSweet shelves plans to build plant in
Quebec *G&M* Jl 7'87 pB1
Saving elusive as sweetener issue sours *VS*
Jl 7'87 pD11
Price drop unlikely for low-cal goods ◆ *CH*
Jl 13'87 pC1
Safety of aspartame doubted in US survey of
69 scientists *G&M* Jl 23'87 pA13
NutraSweet may help women stay on diets say
US researchers MG O 7'87 pG13
Study finds no evidence that sweetener harmful
CH N 5'87 pB13

Aspirin
See also Analgesics
An Aspirin a day cuts risk of stroke major
study shows *TS* F 27'87 pA13
ASA warning delayed by industry, MD says
G&M Ag 10'87 pA10
There's plenty we don't know about ASA
Seiden (C) MG Ag 8'87 pK3

Assassination
Editor who exposed Iran arms deal gunned
down *TS* S 15'87 pA13
Manson disciple (Lynette Fromme) caught after
escape from prison ● *CH* O 26'87
pA9

Assault *See* Crime and criminals -- Assault

Assertiveness
Course in chutzpah gives hope to timid MG
Ja 3'87 pH4

Assessment
See also Property tax
Halifax County assessment figures up 43.6% for
1987 *HCH* Ja 15'87 p13
Evaluation notice can tell a lot: details may
provide grounds to appeal (Winnipeg)
assessor's conclusions ◆ *WFP*
Ja 17'87 p4
Reassessment notices only part of (Winnipeg)
tax picture *WFP* Ja 17'87 p4
(Winnipeg) swamped by assessment appeals
WFP Ja 17'87 p1,4
Property assessment appeals no greater than
normal year *WFP* Jl 7'87 p16
Assessment pits neighbor against neighbor *WFP*
F 18'87 p1
(Winnipeg) taxpayers urge assessment tied to
property value *WFP* S 3'87 p2
Court upholds (Winnipeg's) 1975 base for
assessment *WFP* S 9'87 p3
Property tax woes laid at province's doorstep
CH S 19'87 pA1,A2
Doer gives (Winnipeg) 1988 deadline for
assessment *WFP* N 12'87 p3
North York-Toronto coalition likely to defeat tax
scheme *G&M* N 19'87 pA21
Flynn dismayed by new hurdle facing tax
assessment scheme *G&M* N 20'87 pA16
Property assessment appeals may boost Halifax
tax rate ◆ *HCH* D 1'87 pA7
Homeowners fail to force reassessment *WFP*
D 9'87 p3

● Photograph with article. # Graphic illustration with article. (C) Regular column.
(F) Feature article (Ed) Editorial (L) Letter to the editor (N) Noteworthy article
*CP NewsFile article
CANADIAN NEWS INDEX   See Personal Name Index for information on individuals   1987

Figure 12.4   From the *Canadian News Index*

1004   PERSONAL NAME INDEX

Mulroney, Brian (cont'd)
Angry Nova Scotia workers snub
  PM ●+ MG O 24'87
  pA8
Angry protesters greet PM
  ● HCH O 24'87 p1,2
Hope for Trenton - PM: Mulroney
  seeks "permanent solution" for
  rail car works HCH O 24'87
  p1,2
Mila's man: [excerpt from Friends
  in High Places] ●(F)
  MG O 24'87 pB5
Ugly Halifax protest forces PM to
  retreat G&M O 24'87 pA1,A2
Workers jeer PM [Mulroney] in
  Halifax CH O 24'87 pA3
Workers snub Mulroney
  ●+ WFP O 24'87
  p12
Worker demonstrations too nasty
  - McGillivray (C) CH O 26'87
  pA4
Assault on PM unfair, says MLA
  HCH O 27'87 p1,20
Pawley questions integrity of
  [Mulroney] over Devine "favor"
  WFP O 27'87 p1,4
PM defends 500 Club meeting
  ● HCH O 28'87 p4
Mulroney finds not-so-strange
  bedfellow - Chambers (C) MG
  O 29'87 pB3
Mulroney in not water among
  voters at home ● CH
  O 3'87 pA10
PM tries to counter Sept-lies
  protest ●+ HCH
  O 3'87 p69
PM's failed promises prompt
  protest in his own riding TS
  O 3'87 pA3
[Sept-lies] holds Mulroney to jobs
  vow ●+ WFP
  N 1'87 p9
Third of town shows scorn for
  Mulroney + CH N 1'87
  pA1,A2
Town vents anger at MP
  Mulroney + SS N 1'87 pA7
7,000 march in Sept lies to
  pressure Mulroney ●
  MG N 2'87 pA1,A5
PM's riding outraged:
  demonstrators demand tax credit
  for Sept-lies + HCH N 2'87
  p1,2
Mulroney finally finds his political
  Jeeves ● TS N 7'87
  p04
Patchwork welcome met for PM:
  good news for Trenton awaited
  ● HCH N 16'87 p1,14
Mulroney trades bravado for
  courage - O'Callaghan
  ●(C)(F) CH N 17'87
  pA5
PM empty-handed for Pictou visit
  HCH N 17'87 p1,24
Mulroney stirs crowd in Nova
  Scotia with hints of election MG
  N 18'87 pB1
Pension scheme helps PM defuse
  riding protests TS N 18'87 pA8
Pictou County welcomes PM $8m
  Clearwater expansion to be
  announced - Mulroney
  ● HCH N 18'87 p1,24
PM announces pension for NS
  workers G&M N 18'87 pA8
MP [Fulton] withdraws "lying
  scum" charge after Mulroney
  chastised + WFP N 19'87
  p23
[Mulroney] mends fences in home
  riding + WFP N 19'87 p15
PM attacks foes in election
  tune-up (F) TS N 19'87 pA1,A9
PM slams Liberal senators HCH
  N 19'87 p1,2
Mulroney returns as the candidate
  VS N 21'87 pB1,B2
Base-comeau boy loved at home
  + HCH N 23'87 p18

Mulroney, Brian (cont'd)
[Hoy's] portrait shows PM's warts,
  nothing else - Johnson (C) MG
  N 26'87 pB3
Is Mulroney becoming another
  Pierre Trudeau? WFP N 28'87
  p7
Broadbent rouses BC labor
  meeting by slamming Tories and
  Vander Zalm + MG D 2'87
  pB6
PM rarely holds meet with press
  + WFP D 6'87 p13
Why didn't Mulroney's alarms
  start ringing about Stevens? -
  Winsor (C) G&M D 7'87 pA2
Brian Mulroney as student
  agitator: ah, but that was an
  earlier invention - Lamb (C) VS
  D 18'87 pB9
Ever loyal, Devine stands by his
  PM ● G&M D 21'87
  pA5
Mulroney defends statement on
  Israeli violence. + CH D 23'87
  pA3
American fashion foundation
  awards Mulroney best-dressed
  distinction for conservative style
  WFP D 29'87 p11
Fashion foundation says sartorial
  splendor Mulroney's long suit TS
  D 29'87 pA21
Mulroney makes best-dressed list
  ● G&M D 29'87 pA1
Mulroney scores with Gucci shoes
  HCH D 29'87 p1
Poll gives PM grade C for
  leadership + HCH D 29'87
  p4
Middle East swamp tempts
  another PM VS D 30'87 pB11
Scandal killed PM's hopes in
  early '87 G&M D 31'87 pA5

Mulroney, Mila
First ladies join [Brookfield High]
  school's drug abuse session
  + WFP Ap 7'87 p14
Students greet leaders' wives
  ●+ CH Ap 7'87
  pA3
Quarrel, threats apparently ended
  designer's business with
  Mulroneys G&M Ap 16'87 pA5
Mila's message is "Read, write
  and learn" ● TS
  Je 26'87 pD16
Immigrant interference laid to Mila
  VS S 3'87 pA1
Mila accused of helping immigrant
  teacher "jump queue" TS
  S 4'87 pA1,A8
PMO eased [Grossmann]
  residency bid, letters show
  ●+ WFP S 4'87
  p1,4
PM's wife at centre of charges
  + HCH S 4'87 p1
PM's wife interfered in
  immigration case, union says
  G&M S 4'87 pA5
PM's wife intervened on
  immigration to speed case:
  union ●+ MG
  S 4'87 pA1,A2
PM's [Mulroney] wife intervened
  for teacher + CH S 4'87 pA1
Insults fly in House over Mila
  ● VS S 10'87 pA1
Probe request to immigration by
  Mulroney's wife, MPs demand
  ●+ MG S 10'87
  pB1
Silent PM [Mulroney] watches as
  fight rages over Mila's letter CH
  S 10'87 pA3
Mila's been victimized by her
  husband's government - Nichols
  (C) VS S 11'87 pH8
Mila's missive gives ammunition
  to opposition critics VS S 12'87
  pB3
Mulroney's wife acted properly
  CH S 13'87 pB2

Mulroney, Mila (cont'd)
influence of PM's wife in
  immigration cases sparks
  gratitude, anger ●+
  WFP S 14'87 p1,4
MPs want Mila investigated +
  CH S 15'87 pA3
Probe into Mrs Mulroney's role in
  teacher case blocked by Tories
  G&M O 2'87 pA4
Tories quash probe of Mulroney
  teacher MG O 2'87 pB1
Mila's man: [excerpt from Friends
  in High Places] ●(F)
  MG O 24'87 pB5
Mila Mulroney emerges as very
  political wife ●(F) CH
  D 8'87 pA5
[Susan Riley] book's jibes at Mila
  unconvincing - Triguero (C) CH
  D 11'87 pA4
Political wives: marketing Brian's
  dream (F) TS D 14'87 pB1,B3

Mulvihill, Daniel J
Obituary: former head of Windsor
  university ● TS
  Ja 24'87 pA15

Mulvihill, Paul
Obituary: founded TV ad firm
  ● TS My 30'87 pA14

Munce, Agnes
Albertan celebrates 110th birthday
  ● CH Ja 18'87 pA2

Munday, David
Daredevil [Munday,] police make
  deal on Niagara Falls stunt
  charges + WFP O 13'87 p51
Daredevil is outdone by kayaker
  + G&M O 14'87 pA15
Man paddles Niagara rapids in
  plastic canoe + TS O 14'87
  pA2
New king of Niagara River shoots
  rapids in plastic boat + WFP
  O 14'87 p20

Mundviller, Stephane
Flatfoot flap: suit makes would-be
  cop and MUC fallen-arch
  enemies MG O 31'87 pA3

Munro, Alice
Third Governor-General's award
  for Munro VS My 27'87 pD10
Governor General's Award to
  Munro amid poetry protest
  ●+ MG My 28'87
  pC1
Munro short story collection wins
  award + WFP My 29'87 p34

Munro, Jack
Munro mulls entering NDP
  leadership contest VS Ja 12'87
  pA2
Munro candidacy viewed as
  disaster VS Ja 13'87 pA4
Munro has right stuff to lead
  NDP, Skelly says VS Ja 14'87
  pA12
Munro decides against NDP bid
  VS Ja 19'87 pA3

Munro, John
John Munro wants to run for
  Liberals in Toronto + TS
  Je 18'87 pA20
Munro plans to seek
  [Broadview-Greenwood] Liberal
  nomination ●+ WFP
  Je 18'87 p18
Munro to seek nomination for
  next election + MG
  Je 18'87 pB5
Ex-Liberal minister says party is
  "drifting" + VS
  Je 23'87 pB6
Had nomination within grasp,
  Liberal warhorse steps aside
  G&M O 23'87 pA4

Munro, Lily
Thoroughly modern Lily [Lily
  Munro] ● G&M
  Mr'87 (Toronto) p40-43+

Munsch, Robert
The world according to Munsch
  ●(F) G&M Ja 24'87
  pE1
Subversion is his schtik
  ● WFP My 27'87 p36
The raconteur of the day-care set
  ●(F) G&M My 27'87 pd1
Robert Munsch readying sore
  tonsils for Montreal shows
  ● MG O 22'87 pC1
Stage is Munsch's desk for
  rewrites WFP N 26'87 p81

Murphy, Eddie
Eddie's second-coming: plenty of
  hoopla for Murphy's law, Part II
  ● MG My 19'87 pF1

Murphy, Joan
Hot new faces: up and coming
  talents ● WFP
  Ap 4'87 p19,20

Murphy, Joe
It used to be so easy for Joe
  Murphy TS Mr 9'87 pB4

Murphy, Kevin
BC Place chief named + WFP
  My 16'87 p16
Both school boards select new
  chairmen ●(F) CH
  O 27'87 pA5

Murphy, Linda K
Ottawa's Linda Murphy judges
  what's obscene and what isn't
  G&M Ag 15'87 pC1

Murphy, Peter
Enraging Canadians just a job for
  envoy G&M Ja 31'87 pD3

Murphy, Turk
Obituary: jazz trombonist MG
  Je 2'87 pD9
Obituary: San Francisco
  trombonist became a jazz
  legend G&M Je 3'87 pA17

Murray, Anne
Murray's career still soaring after
  taking off with Snowbird
  ● WFP F 25'87 p35
Canada's songbird [Anne Murray]
  flies coast to coast
  ●(F) TS Mr 28'87
  pJ1
Anne Murray to kick off Canada
  tour on prairies + VS
  Ap 4'87 pE2
Murray begins first cross-Canada
  tour in 17 years + HCH
  Ap 4'87 p41
Anne's out to enjoy her success
  ● CH Ap 10'87 pE1
On the road again [Anne Murray]
  ● MG My 2'87 pG1
Anne's [Murray] still pushing for
  big bucks TS My 5'87 pE1
Murray's timeless voice soars
  over frustrations ●
  G&M My 13'87 pC6
Singing star donates $100,000 for
  hospital upgrading +
  HCH My 27'87 p29
Murray finds harmony with fame
  ● MG My 28'87
  p1-O,3-O
Springhill facility to house Anne
  Murray memorabilia ●
  HCH Je 6'87 p33
Murray's homecoming no letdown,
  for Anne or fans ●
  HCH Je 8'87 p1-E
Top-quality songs, unique voice
  carry Murray to top WFP
  O 11'87 p17

●Photograph with article. #Graphic Illustration with article. (C)Regular column.
(F)Feature article (Ed)Editorial (L)Letter to the editor (N)Noteworthy article
+CP NewsFile article
See Subject Index for information by Subject

1987   CANADIAN NEWS INDEX

Figure 12.5 From the *Canadian Business Index*

28 SUBJECT INDEX

Automation (cont'd)
The automation triangle new paths to productivity performance # *Business Quarterly* 52(2) S'87 p61-67
Report on the office and computers: special report *Globe & Mail* N 16'87 pC1-C24

Automation and labor
See also Technological change
Success belongs to workers whose training and education allow them to apply new technology ● *OA Office Mgt & Automation* 2(12) D'86 p44-48+
Tech change: boon or bane for professionals, supervisors and middle managers *Cdn Public Administration* 29(4) Wint'86 p562-566
Automation hits at middle classes *Northern Ont Business* 7(4) Ja'87 p19
Microelectronics: not as guilty as charged *Worklife* 5(2) Mr'87 p10-11
Productivity, wages, higher with high-tech change *Worklife* 5(2) Mr'87 p17
... world *OA Office M*...

Automobile dealers (cont'd)
Megadealer concept gaining momentum *Financial Post* 81(8) F 23'87 p36
Selling the salesman ● *Metro Toronto Business* 77(5) Je'87 p9
Number [one] Vaughn [Wyant] Jubilee Ford's youthful president ● *Saskatchewan Business* 8(9) O'87 p16-18
Car dealer loses challenge to probe of selling practices *Globe & Mail* D 9'87 pA13
Consumers reimbursed by Vehicle Compensation Fund *Protect Yourself* D'87 p9

Advertising

See Automobiles - Advertising

New Brunswick

Auto makers angry about New Brunswick [car dealer] law *Globe & Mail* N 12'87 pB1,B4

Automobile drivers *See* Drivers and driving

Automobile engines
See also Tru...

Automobile engines (cont'd)

Testing

Testing for cylinder balance on computer controlled engines # *Service Station & Garage Mgt* 17(3) Mr'87 p25-26
[Varity Corp says its Perkins Engines unit's new turbocharged diesel engine for medium-duty commercial vehicles has passed US emissions tests] *Globe & Mail* S 26'87 pB12

Automobile expenses *See* Business expenses -- Automobiles

Automobile industry
Strong public support for Canadian content in autos *Cdn Labour* 31(7) S'86 p5
Auto industry: special report # ● *Financial Post* 81(8) F 23'87 p33-38
Car capacity crisis revs up: global competition key industry issue *Financial Post* 81(8) F 23'87 p33
...poses problems for...

CORPORATE NAME INDEX 639

General Motors Corp. ●● (cont'd)
GM expands its division for Cadillacs *Globe & Mail* Ja 9'87 pB5
Volvo, GM tackle heavy truck market *Globe & Mail* Ja 10'87 pB6
Greyhound set to buy GM bus-making plants *Globe & Mail* Ja 13'87 pB2
GM's luxury Allante essential for prestige *Globe & Mail* Ja 16'87 pB15
GM to outline Perot buyout *Globe & Mail* Ja 28'87 pB17
GM expected to drive US auto profits lower *Globe & Mail* Ja 29'87 pB4
GM may buy more shares *Glo*...
...'87 pB4

General Motors Corp. ●● (cont'd)
Pair shares GM inventor awards *Financial Post* 81(20) My 18'87 p38
GM division makes cutbacks *Globe & Mail* My 20'87 pB3
GM head keeps his cool under holders' fire *Globe & Mail* My 23'87 pB13
GM Saturn: from main ring to sideshow *Globe & Mail* My 29'87 pB1,B2
GM's shiny Spanish plant beset by labor strife *Globe & Mail* Je 23'87 pB25
GM, Boeing and Ford head US exporters *Globe & Mail* Jl 2'87 pB10
GM finds ... its market share diffic...

General Motors Corp. ●● (cont'd)
GM takes long-range view on regaining market share *Globe & Mail* N 16'87 pB18
Cadillac's new spirit willing but flashy car's sales weak [Cadillac] *Globe & Mail* N 17'87 pB15
Harder arteries a problem for GM # *Globe & Mail* N 23'87 pB1,B9
Toyota and GM said set to merge subsidiaries operating in Australia *Globe & Mail* N 25'87 pB22
Million funds putting millions in buyout fund *Globe & Mail* D 3'87 pB12
Moody's reviewing rating for GM's long-term debt *Globe & Mail* D 5'87 pB9
...will be over by 199...

PERSONAL NAME INDEX 1043

Smed, Mogens
Author: After bankruptcy: how you revive your business after it's gone bankrupt *Alberta Business* 4(3) My/Je'87 p27-29

Smil, Vaclav
Author: China and Japan in the new energy era *Jnl Business Admin* 16(1-2) 1986 p223-233

Smillie, Elizabeth
Author: Cultivating hope: Agdevco in Africa ● *Saskatchewan Business* 8(7) Jl/Ag'87 p42-48

Smit, Guido
Bell Technical Services Inc appointment ● *Globe & Mail* Ag 27'87 pB9

Smith, Colin E
British Columbia Chamber of Commerce election *CIM Bulletin* 80(905) S'87 p29

Smith, David
Will stew over auditors boil? [reactions to Estey report] ● *Bottom Line* Ja'87 p8-9
Author: Debate desired on CA monopoly issue *Financial Post* 81(8) F 23'87 p8

Smith, Derek
Eight of the best [mutual fund managers] # ● *Your Money* 3(1) F'87 p44-46+

Smith, Don
Ellis-Don chief watching Ontario election race closely ● *Financial Post* 81(36) S 7'87 p8

Smith, Donald C
Oilweek's cartoonist finally comes in from the cold ● *Oilweek* 38(9) Mr 30'87 p17

Smith, Donna
Trail-blazing entrepreneurs look to fill sports medicine niche [Achilles Sports Medicine Shop] ● *Sports Business* 14(10) D'86 p6-7

Smith, Doug
These are the ones to watch for ... le 22'87

Smith, HW
Author: Upgrading of aluminum dross by selective comminution and sizing # ● *CIM Bulletin* 80(900) Ap'87 p73-78

Smith, Jack
Westar Mining appointment *Northern Miner* 72(43) Ja 5'87 p5

Smith, John D
Author: Centrifuge model studies for backfill design at Westmin Resources Ltd. HW Mine # ● *CIM Bulletin* 80(903) Jl'87 p39-44

Smith, JW
Rotten-eggs gas given a breath of fresh air *Globe & Mail* D 29'87 pB2

Smith, L Graham
Author: Reforming the federal environmental assessment and review process *Cdn Public Policy* 12(4) D'86 p596-605

Smith, Larry D
Author: Inflation in project evaluation: mineral economics # ● *CIM Bulletin* 80(899) Mr'87 p129-133
Author: Using partnerships as tax-planning vehicles *CA Magazine* 120(7) Jl'87 p36-38

Smith, Michael
Author: So long glue pot, hello desktop *Bus to Bus Marketing* 3(2) Je 29'87 pB1,B12
[New Brunswick prospector of the year] *Northern Miner* 73(19) Jl 20'87 p6

Smith, Murray
Author: [Global Imbalances And US Policy Responses: A Canadian Perspective] BR *CA Magazine* 120(9) S'87 p26
Editor: [Policy Harmonization: The Effect Of A Canadian American Free Trade Area] BR *Cdn Public Policy* 13(3) S'87 p397-398
Telephony Communications International Inc appointment ● *Globe & Mail* O 17'87 pB5

Smith, Nancy J

Smith, Philip (cont'd)
Business book award winner *Quill & Quire* 53(7) Jl'87 p54

Smith, Prior
Prior Smith fills US airwaves with Canadian news ● *Your Money* 3(8) O'87 p8,9

Smith, Raymond
Canadian Imperial Bank of Commerce appointment ● *Financial Post* 81(46) N 16'87 p17
Canadian Imperial Bank of Commerce appointment ● *Globe & Mail* N 17'87 pB13

Smith, Robert M
American Barrick Resources Corp appointment ● *Financial Post* 81(35) Ag 31'87 p18
American Barrick Resources Corp appointment ● *Globe & Mail* S 1'87 pB18
American Barrick Resources Corp appointment ● *Northern Miner* 73(26) S 7'87 p2
American Barrick Resources Corp appointment ● *Financial Post* 81(36) S 7'87 p4

Smith, Robert S
Canada Plastic Containers Ltd appointment *Cdn Packaging* 40(1) Ja'87 p128

Smith, Robin B
John Labatt appointment ● *Globe & Mail* O 23'87 pB7
John Labatt Ltd appointment ● *Financial Post* 81(44) N 2'87 p14
John Labatt Ltd appointment ● *Financial Times* 76(20) N 2'87 p4-5

Smith, Roderick
Author: [Gold Situation - 1987] BR *Northern Miner* 73(36) N 16'87 pB16

Smith, Roger
Under siege, GM chairman starts fighting back *Globe & Mail* Mr 10'87 pB19

Smith, Roland
Film vp sells [Montreal] cinema ... *Mediascene* 6(4)...

Smith, Stuart (cont'd)
Science Council chairman to be technology-financing consultant *Globe & Mail* Mr 25'87 pB4
Fanning the flames of entrepreneurial fire: roundtable of opportunity ● *Small Business* 6(6) Je'87 p57-60

Smith, Sylvia
Author: Major revisions to the [CICA] handbook's auditing volume *CA Magazine* 120(8) Ag'87 p69-70+

Smithson, Erin
Author: Paintin' the town red [Computer Color Matching System] *Manitoba Business* Jl/Ag'87 p60-62

Smyth, Stan M
Valmet Automation appointment ● *Globe & Mail* N 25'87 pB15

Smyth, Tom
Three to receive 1986 Gold Pencils *Cdn Grocer* 100(8) Ag'86 p107
Graham, Herrick, Smyth are honored: Knights of the Golden Pencil, 1986, saluted by industry ● *Cdn Grocer* 101(1) Ja'87 p26,27

Smythe, Hugh
Author: Downhill battle: the battlefields are the mountain slopes, the weapons, anything that works ● *BC Business* 15(3) Mr'87 p44-49

Snaith, Victor
Zeta function problem solved # ● *Cdn Research* 20(6) Je'87 p28

Sneath, Allen
Sneath starts own consultancy service ● *Marketing* 91(13) Mr 30'87 p3

Snelgrove, Tim
A new recipe for retailing ● *Metro Toronto Business* 77(7) S'87 p9

Snell, James G
Author: [The Supreme Court Of Canada: History Of The Institution] BR *Cdn Public Administration* 30(1) Spr'87 p127-128

In most instances, the information specialist operating the centre will provide you with free consulting services to narrow down or refine your request. This will save you time and money as the staff bring their experience and knowledge to bear in a sometimes complex process.

You may decide, after using computer services at the library, that you want to start your own centre. This would be a practical step for any business requiring daily information. The cost to achieve this on a modest scale will start at about $3,000. This figure includes the cost of an IBM-compatible personal computer, a printer, some basic software, and a telephone. The telephone is hooked up to a "modem," a device which translates computer signals over the telephone.

You will also be billed for each withdrawal from a database. The cost varies considerably, depending on the time of day or night of the withdrawal and the length of time required to process the information request. The more experienced you become with computer searches, the cheaper the cost. Some database vendors have made searches relatively easy, while those of others are very sophisticated and require training.

As stated, you don't need to own a computer to get at the information. Some database vendors will provide you with custom-made searches and will mail you a paper copy of the results. Still, your best buy remains at the public library.

There is a wonderful range of computer data. Let's look at some specific examples. My first appreciation for on-line searches began a few years ago while making a guest appearance on CBC's national radio program, "Morningside." As mentioned at the beginning of this book, I was assigned a series of research problems, including the compilation of a list of Canadian companies which had a direct financial interest in South Africa. One logical first step in tackling this problem was to sift through *Inter-Corporate Ownership*, carefully searching for Canadian firms which had offices in South Africa. Given the staggering number of entries listed in microscopic type in this telephone directory-sized book, the task would have taken six months and left me with severe eye strain. However, a relatively simple on-line search offered through Canada Systems Group's database, "Inter-Corporate Ownership," yielded the necessary results. And it took less than two minutes!

My own question was, of course, merely one of an infinite variety of research questions which can be answered effortlessly through on-line searches.

You may be researching a person, such as Stephen Overbury, and want to assemble a list of the kinds of articles he has written. One way to achieve a partial list is to link up to the on-line version of the *Canadian Periodical Index*, offered through Info Globe. As you can see in Figure 12.6, various citations appear. You could find copies of these magazines in most larger public libraries if you wanted to read entire articles.

Some databases reprint the *full text* of articles. For example, if you were researching the topic of senior citizens in universities, you might look for examples in newspapers. One of several databases to solve this information request is the on-line version of the *Globe and Mail*. By searching under either of the subject headings, "Aged Persons," "University Degrees," "Adult Education," "Student Graduates," or under the name of the graduate or writer of the article, you would be able to access the full text of the story of an 82-year-old graduate, which appears in figure 12.7.

My favourite example of the obviously beneficial uses of the computer for research purposes involves Dr. Timothy Murray, a Professor of Medicine at the University of Toronto and an expert in bone and mineral deficiencies. Dr. Murray's portable laptop computer proved indispensable in completing a medical book. It enabled him to do research day or night, at home, at the library, or at the cottage—wherever he had access to a telephone. With a telephone and modem, he was able to tap into MEDLINE, the database of the U.S. National Library of Medicine, which maintains close to 4.3 million references to biomedical journal articles from over 3,500 journals published in 71 countries. What a powerful source!

Figure 12.8 reproduces a sample search, under the topic of bone and mineral deficiencies, illustrating an abstract of a study found in MEDLINE.

With an estimated 5,000 commercial databases in existence and a growth rate of 500 bases each year, selecting the most appropriate base can become overwhelming, to say the least. This is why I strongly recommend examining the following list of useful reference materials, each of which will enhance your life with computers:

- *Business Online: The Canadian Professional's Guide To Electronic Information Sources* (John Wiley and Sons) is an incredible undertaking. It was co-ordinated under the skillfull guidance of experienced on-line researchers and librarians, Ulla de Stricker, of Micromedia Limited and Jane Dysart of the Royal Bank. This is a thorough "how to" book which takes you step-by-step through your own on-line searches. Topics cover the evaluation of on-line searches and the details of communications software. Case studies make this an even more meaningful book. The text includes an important section on key Canadian databases, particularly as they relate to business topics.

- *The Espial Canadian Database Directory* (Espial Productions, P.O. Box 624, Station "K", Toronto, Ontario M4P 2H1). This superb 33-page booklet, which is handily indexed, documents useful data on 215 crucial databases. The compiler, H.C. Campbell, has carefully prepared a practical and necessary listing of the approximate Canadian content in each database.

- *Databook Directory of OnLine Services* (McGraw-Hill Information Systems). This mammoth two-volume, loose-leaf service covers Canadian and foreign databases and profiles the database vendors themselves. Updated regularly, it appears to be one of the most extensive lists of bases in existence.

- *Canadian Machine Readable Databases: A Directory and Guide,* compiled by Helen Rogers for the National Library of Canada. Lists the full names of Canadian databases, subject(s) and other important information.

- *Database Canada* is a bi-monthly Canadian newsletter (available by writing to 346 Brookdale Avenue, Toronto, Ontario M5M 1P8). Edited by two librarians, Beverley Watters and Jacqueline Halupke, it monitors Canadian databases and foreign vendors to evaluate their Canadian content. The newsletters also offer software and hardware tips to help users overcome the quirks of most systems.

In addition to these reference materials, it is just as advisable to write to the individual database vendors directly and request information kits. The above mentioned book, *Business OnLine*, and various computer magazines and directories, provide the addresses of a large number of these vendors in Canada.

Locating Publications and Libraries   Most larger libraries carry a healthy collection of serials, including the publications discussed earlier in this chapter under "Periodical Indexes." If your library doesn't subscribe to the publications you seek, locate a library that does by referring to the publication, *Union List of Serials in the Social Sciences and Humanities Held by Canadian Libraries*, published by the National Library of Canada. Then arrange an interlibrary loan through your local library or visit the library that owns the periodical.

Figure 12.6 Sample of Info Globe's on-line version of *Canadian Periodical Index*, showing citations of articles

```
DATAPAC: call connected to 3950 0032
         (005) (n, remote charging, packet size: 256)

INFO GLOBE DATABASE - PLEASE SIGN ON: inf04/pi
JULY 28, 1988 11:10
CANADA NEWS-WIRE SPECIAL OFFER - ?NEWS FOR DETAILS

Welcome to the Canadian Periodical Index Online
Contains issues from January 1977 to July 4 1988. The default
date range is January 1987 to date. Type SETR to change the
range. All material covered by copyright
  CPI ONLINE SEARCH MENU
Canadian Thesaurus now available - call Info Globe to order
your copy

1. Change the date range
2. Search for a word or words IN THE TITLE
3. Articles about a specific COMPANY or ORGANIZATION
4. Articles about a specific SUBJECT or subjects
5. Articles ABOUT a specific PERSON
6. Articles BY a specific PERSON
7. Articles BY OR ABOUT a specific PERSON
8. Articles that appeared in a specific PERIODICAL or
   periodicals
9. SEARCH WITHOUT MENUS (FREE TEXT SEARCH)

Enter selection number, OFF - leave system
> 9
ENTER QUERY
> setr all
Range from Jan.01,1977 to Dec.02,1988
ENTER QUERY
> stephen overbury
PROCEEDING
Search Processed
Proximity search - - 1 Document Found - - 6 Documents not yet
scanned
Enter an Info Globe display command OR
Type A - SCAN, B - Send Continuously, C - Other Commands, X-
EXIT, - - Full reply list
> pc all
CPI ONLINE - Document 1 - 6 left to scan
TITLE      :   Finding Canadian facts fast
SOURCE     :   Canadian Author & Bookman
VOLUME     :   62 no 3
DATE       :   April 1987
PAGE       :   25
AUTHOR     :   *Stephen*Overbury*
SAUTHOR    :   Overbury
SUBJECT    :   Book reviews; Reference books

CPI ONLINE - Document 2 - 5 left to scan
TITLE      :   Finding Canadian facts fast
SOURCE     :   Books in Canada
VOLUME     :   15
DATE       :   January-February 1986
PAGE       :   24
AUTHOR     :   *Stephen*Overbury*
SAUTHOR    :   Overbury
SUBJECT    :   Book reviews

CPI ONLINE - Document 3 - 4 left to scan
TITLE      :   Finding Canadian facts fast
SOURCE     :   Quill & Quire
VOLUME     :   51
```

```
DATE        :   June 1985
PAGE        :   40
AUTHOR      :   *Stephen*Overbury*
SAUTHOR     :   Overbury
SUBJECT     :   Book reviews

CPI ONLINE - Document 4 - 3 left to scan
TITLE       :   In the hierarchy of backroom boys, Charles
                McMillan is numero uno for the Tories
SOURCE      :   Canadian Business
VOLUME      :   57
DATE        :   January 1984
PAGE        :   37
AUTHOR      :   *Stephen*Overbury*
SAUTHOR     :   Overbury
SUBJECT
 PERSON     :   Charles J. McMillan
ILLUS       :   il part

CPI ONLINE - Document 5 - 2 left to scan
TITLE       :   Blood money: Canadian firms make a fortune
                selling "civilian" arms used by repressive
                regimes
SOURCE      :   Today
DATE        :   December 12 1981
PAGE        :   p8-8a-8b, 16
AUTHOR      :   *Stephen*Overbury*
SAUTHOR     :   Overbury
SUBJECT     :   MUNITIONS; ARMS trade
ILLUS       :   il

CPI ONLINE - Document 6 - 1 left to scan
TITLE       :   Detroit vs. the imports: how they rate in the
                small-car class
SOURCE      :   Canadian Business
VOLUME      :   54
DATE        :   March 1981
PAGE        :   151, 153
AUTHOR      :   *Stephen*Overbury*
SAUTHOR     :   Overbury
SUBJECT     :   AUTOMOBILES - Testing
ILLUS       :   il tabs

CPI ONLINE - Document 7 of 7
TITLE       :   Sue and be dandy
SOURCE      :   Books in Canada
VOLUME      :   9
DATE        :   November 1980
PAGE        :   3-6
AUTHOR      :   *Stephen*Overbury*
SAUTHOR     :   Overbury
SUBJECT     :   LIBEL and slander; DEFAMATION
ILLUS       :   il

END OF PRINT
Type A-SCAN, B-Send Continuously, C-Other Commands, X-EXIT, ?-
Full reply list
> off

                         DATABASE USAGE
   DATABASE   CONNECT TIME SEARCHES DISPLAYS   SORTS   KEY ITEMS
      CPI          2          1        7         0
SIGNOFF REQUEST ACCEPTED.                                LINES
CONNECT TIME - 0:02 AT 11:11 ON JULY 28, 1988
```

Figure 12.7   Sample printout of the on-line version of the *Globe and Mail*, showing full text of an article

```
            ** Convocation at 82 **
          ** Oldest graduate was told **
          ** she'd never read again **
               By STEPHEN OVERBURY

   The oldest graduate ever to earn a Bachelor of Arts*degree* at
the University of Toronto was once told she would never read
another book.
   Doctors predicted blindness for Gladys*Jennings*of Toronto 15
years ago. But her eyes held up and, on Wednesday, the 82-year-
old woman will join 2,000 other students to receive her general
three-year BA at the university's convocation.
   "I always wanted to go to university," she said during a
recent break from writing an essay for another course. "I
couldn't as a mother and then it wasn't important to go to
school . . . there weren't the opportunities for women. You
either worked in an office, a factory or as a nurse. There are
many, many senior citizens today that are capable of returning
to school. They just need a little encouragement."
   Mrs. *Jennings* began her working life as a proofreader for
Maclean Publishing Co., where her father had a job. Thinking
she could put her high school diploma and business school
training to better use, she switched jobs and became a
stenographer, but regretted it.
   "Proofreading was a better job. But I was young and idealistic
and felt there was more security in being a stenographer," she
said.
   She left Maclean to marry and raise two children. Later she
joined the federal civil service as a stenographer, where she
worked until retirement in 1961.
   Ten years later she began studying at the University of
Toronto's Woodsworth College, before a free tuition program for
senior citizens was established.
   Anthropology is her favorite subject. "I'd like to know about
the beginnings of the world. Who were the first people on this
hemisphere- I haven't found that out for certain," she said.
   Her west Toronto residence is cluttered with books, but no
television: "I haven't the time for it."
   Did her recollection of important events of the past help in
her academic career- Not really, she said. There's so much you
can't write about (in essays). I was very much alive in the
Winnipeg General Strike (in 1919) but I didn't think much of it
at the time. I had my own home to look after. Just because I
lived then doesn't mean I could write 3,500 words on it."
   This year, Mrs. *Jennings* reduced her yearly load of two
courses to one - a study of working-class history in Canada.
"It's really a course about the left," she said. "But I'm not
that way."
   The course will be counted toward a four-year*degree,*which
requires five credits more than the 15 she has now.
   Mrs.*Jennings*maintains membership in several organizations,
including the Business and Professional Women's Club which, she
said, looks after the interests of women. "We lobby legislation
through Parliament . . . women can keep up to men."
ADDED SEARCH TERMS: aged persons university degrees adult
education students graduates.

END OF PRINT
Type A-SCAN, B-Send Continuously, C-Other Commands, X-EXIT, ?-
Full reply list
> off
                        DATABASE USAGE
   DATABASE   CONNECT TIME SEARCHES DISPLAYS   SORTS  KEY ITEMS
      GAM          2           1       7          0
SIGNOFF REQUEST ACCEPTED.                               LINES
CONNECT TIME - 0:02 AT 9:38 ON JULY 27, 1988
```

Figure 12.8   Sample printout of an on-line MEDLINE search, showing an abstract of a study

```
bone a # d bones and explode *minerals
PROG:
SS (6) PSTG (302)

SS 7/C?
USER:
prt ar comp - 21
PROG:

21
UI - 88190891
AU - McDermott MT ; Witte MC
TI - Bone mineral content in smokers.
AB - We did a cross-sectional evaluation of the effect of
     heavy cigarette smoking on bone mass using single photon
     absorptiometry (SPA) of the radius in 35 smokers (24
     women, 11 men) and 35 nonsmokers (24 women, 11 men).
     Individuals from the two groups were carefully matched
     for sex, age, weight, height, calcium intake, and, for
     women, menopausal history and estrogen use. We found no
     differences between smokers and nonsmokers at the middle
     or distal portion of the radius. This suggests that
     smoking has no direct effect on appendicular bone mass;
     however, it may still influence bone loss indirectly
     through effects on other factors such as age at
     menopause, body weight, diet, and possibly physical
     activity.
SO - South Med J 1988 Apr;81(4):477-80
```

Various directories help you locate the libraries in your area. For an exhaustive list of these directories, consult the helpful booklet, *Directories of Canadian Libraries* by S. Racine. It's available free of charge from the Library Documentation Centre, National Library of Canada, 395 Wellington Street, Ottawa, Ontario K1A 0N4 (telephone (613) 995-8717).

Also recommended are *The Canadian Library Yearbook* which lists over 6,500 academic, public and special libraries according to location, subject and name, the *Corpus Almanac & Canadian Sourcebook*, and the *Canadian Almanac and Directory*. In addition *The American Library Directory* is especially helpful in that it gives the size of library collections and their budgets (including Canadian libraries), information which can help you determine the likelihood of a library's subscribing to the journals you seek.

Another useful directory to keep in mind when searching for libraries is *Subject Collections: A Guide to Special Book Collections*, edited by Lee Ash. These specialized collections could include copies of obscure publications you might be seeking. For example, if you were researching Sir Arthur Conan Doyle and wanted back copies of *Strand* magazine, in which his early Sherlock Holmes stories first appeared, you would find the listing in this directory for the "Sir Arthur Conan Doyle Collection" in the Metropolitan Toronto Library, which holds these back copies.

If you can't arrange an interlibrary loan, you may have to write directly to the publisher for back copies of a publication. If you need articles or reports listed in any of the indexes published by Micromedia, you can purchase them directly from Micromedia Limited, Document Delivery Service, 158 Pearl Street, Toronto, Ontario M5H 1L3.

Using Libraries to Find Experts   One of the fundamental principles of research is to attempt to acquire the information we need from experts who have already done the research. The trick, of course, is to find the right expert, and for this, too, libraries can be useful. Larger libraries are divided into specialized departments, from business to fine art, and each department keeps professional directories. If, for example, you wanted to find a local expert who could interpret financial data, you would find the latest issue of *The Financial Analysts Federation Membership Directory* in the business department of your library. (*It is always a good practice to refer to the latest issue of any directory, because the information can become outdated quickly.*) Most professional groups, in fact, publish membership directories.

The general reference department of libraries keep the *Directory of Associations in Canada*, which lists about 16,000 international, national, interprovincial, and provincial organizations in Canada. It also provides the association's name, address, elected officials, and information on annual meetings. Each of these associations have members who are experts. If you call the wrong group, chances are you can be referred by them to a more suitable organization.

To supplement this directory, you can conduct a newspaper search; newspapers often quote experts and organizations. It can also be fruitful to check with department heads of libraries, as they usually keep abreast of who is doing research in what field.

Finally, you can contact the editors of trade publications directly. Trade editors, such as those at Maclean Hunter and Southam Communications, are extremely knowledgeable about the information sources, including experts available in their field.

ACADEMIC LIBRARIES

If you and the staff at the reference desk have exhausted every possible source of information available in the public library system, you may find answers to your questions in an academic library. There are a few hundred *college* and *university* libraries in Canada.

The staff at the public library may refer you to either a university or a college library. Some college libraries have extremely sophisticated information sources in some subject areas. For example, if you were researching darkroom techniques, a community college offering programs in this area might very well have a wealth of data. Larger libraries may also have some of this information, but if you live in a remote part of the country, it may be more expedient for you to contact your nearest college library.

Your local library personnel are the key advisers in directing you to outside libraries because they can smooth your path by indicating to the next library that the preliminary search has been done. Have the public library staff call the other library for you and arrange an appointment. For a list of college and university libraries, refer to the *Canadian Library Yearbook*.

SPECIAL LIBRARIES

If, after searching through the public library system and academic libraries, you still haven't solved your information needs, the library personnel may refer you to a special library. Special libraries are not in most instances supported by tax dollars; their main purpose is to meet an organization's internal needs. However, you may be able to gain access to a special library with the help of a referral from the library personnel in the public library system if you have exhausted other possibilities.

The general procedure is to go through your local library because the staff at special libraries are very familiar with the holdings of the public library system. If you request information that is already obtainable in the public system, don't expect a special library to help you.

There are several thousand special libraries in Canada, some of which were formed in the mid-nineteenth century. These include government special libraries. Although government special libraries, too, service their own organizations, they can be a resource, as their personnel may feel obligated to help outsiders because public tax dollars are involved.

To locate the most appropriate special library, refer to the *Canadian Library Yearbook* and examine the subject index of the directory. If you live in Toronto, Montreal, Calgary, or Edmonton, your local public library should keep a directory of all special libraries in your city.

Special libraries do not resemble traditional libraries. Their book collections are often limited, and most of their information comes from periodicals, computer services, and the telephone. The staff at special libraries form a very strong network with each other, particularly when they share similar subject areas. Special library staff have helped each other through tough economic times by offering free advice and exchanging various information services. This network has obvious advantages for you. If you establish contact with one member of the staff at a special library, you are in effect tapping into a wider network.

Employees at many of the special libraries will help you provided you have a legitimate research need that cannot be met by the public library or academic library system. A lot depends on their workload, so it pays to telephone the library first and allow ample time to set up an information search.

SCHOOL LIBRARIES

A school library, which can be found in any elementary or high school, is really just a specialized public library, available to the students who attend that school.

Its collection is established to serve a specific clientele and their needs: students and teachers in either elementary or high schools. As such, the collection will contain all the types of materials found in any good public library that are related to curricular and recreational needs, including

- reference materials, such as general and subject encyclopedias, yearbooks, and dictionaries

- non-print materials such as video and audio tapes, sound recordings, slides, filmstrips, kits, games, and microfilms

- hardback and paperback books

- serials such as magazines and newspapers
- information and picture files
- miscellaneous items, such as maps, globes, and models.

In most provinces, the school library is staffed by one or more trained teacher-librarians, who have taken courses to become both qualified teachers and specialized school librarians. Thus, your school librarian is fully aware of the curriculum taught in your school, the teacher's needs, and the assignments that you will be given. In addition, the librarian is knowledgeable about the types of fiction that will appeal to you. Teacher-librarians work hard to effect a "partnership" between staff, students, and the library in order to encourage and assist in what is known to teachers as "resource-based learning."

If you were to approach the librarian for information and material for an ecology project, you would probably not be given a bibliography or list of specific items. Instead, the librarian would provide a Resource List, like the one shown in Figure 12.9, on the following page. This, of course, is also a research strategy designed to allow you to access information on ecology in any school or public library. Notice that instead of providing specific titles, the school librarian has provided a list of the different *materials* available and specific *subject headings*.

This resource list is both a general summary of the areas of information in the library and a specific guide on accessing the materials by appropriate subject headings designed for the subject of ecology. Once you have mastered this type of approach, it can easily be adopted to any other topic for which you need information or for any subject on which you would like recreation reading.

Figure 12.9   Sample of a school library resource list

```
RESOURCE LIST TO ACCESS MATERIALS ON: ECOLOGY

1.   REFERENCE COLLECTION

     Consult the following types of materials; look in the
     INDEX under the subject headings suggested in 2 below.

     GENERAL ENCYCLOPEDIAS and their YEARBOOKS
     SCIENCE YEARBOOKS
     SCIENCE ENCYCLOPEDIAS
     SCIENCE DICTIONARIES
     CURRENT BIOGRAPHY

2.   BOOK, NON-PRINT, INFORMATION FILE COLLECTIONS
     To locate books, clippings, audio and video tapes,
     filmstrips, etc., look in your SUBJECT CARD CATALOGUE
     under the following subject headings:

     ADAPTATION (BIOLOGY)          MARINE POLLUTION
     AIR-POLLUTION                 NATURAL GAS-PIPELINES
     ANIMALS - GEOGRAPHIC          NATURE CONSERVATION
      DISTRIBUTION                 NOISE POLLUTION
     BOTANY - ECOLOGY              OIL POLLUTION OF WATER
     ECOLOGY                       PESTICIDES
     EVOLUTION                     PESTICIDES-ENVIRONMENTAL
     FISHES-GEOGRAPHICAL            ASPECTS
      DISTRIBUTION                 PESTICIDES AND WILDLIFE
     FOOD ADULTERATION AND         PETROLEUM-PIPELINES
      INSPECTION                   PLANTS-GEOGRAPHICAL
     FOOD CHAINS (ECOLOGY)          DISTRIBUTION
     GENETICS                      POLLUTION
     HUMAN ECOLOGY                 POPULATION
     HYDROELECTRIC POWER PLANTS-    RADIOACTIVE POLLUTION
      CANADA                       TECHNOLOGY AND CIVILIZATION
     JAMES BAY HYDROELECTRIC       VARIATION (BIOLOGY)
      PROJECT                      WATER-POLLUTION
     MACKENZIE VALLEY PIPELINE     WILDLIFE CONSERVATION
     MAN-INFLUENCE OF ENVIRONMENT  SCIENTISTS-BIOGRAPHY See also
     MAN-INFLUENCE ON NATURE        names of individual
     MARINE ECOLOGY                 scientists, e.g., Carson,
                                    Rachel

                                   Also persons, places and
                                    subjects with the
                                    subdivision
                                    FICTION, e.g., ECOLOGY-
                                    FICTION
3.   PERIODICAL COLLECTION

     To locate articles in periodicals or magazines, consult
     the Readers' Guide to Periodical Literature and the
     Canadian Periodical Index under the subject headings
     suggested in 2 above.
```

Accessing Local Government Sources

What is strange about the municipal level of government is that it's usually the most open level, because it's non-partisan. Because of this, it tends to be less difficult to get information.

Barbara Caplan, Deputy Clerk, City of Toronto

Do you want to find out how many dogs Sir John A. Macdonald kept at his house while he lived in Toronto? How about finding the home address of someone who has an unlisted telephone number? Perhaps you want to learn all you can about a proposed development in your neighbourhood? Or you may need to know how much you will be taxed for running a local business.

You can answer all of these questions in a flash by visiting your local government—that is, once you survive a gruelling orientation. Local governments may be the most open form of government, but they also tend to be the most confusing in terms of structure and what information you are legally entitled to.

Many people, including me, have mistakenly thought that "city government" or "city hall" was synonymous with local government. There are, in fact, many other forms of local government. In British Columbia there are six different types of municipal governments, including city governments. In Ontario the structure is even more elaborate, encompassing villages, towns, cities, boroughs, separated towns, townships, improvement districts, police villages, counties, and metropolitan and regional municipalities.

Don't relax yet—that's only the beginning of this myriad. In addition to the various forms of local government, there are also many kinds of local governing bodies or "special-purpose bodies," such as boards and commissions. In Ontario alone, one survey found seventy different types of special-purpose bodies representing two thousand local governing bodies.

Local governments have, in fact, been an organizational nightmare since Confederation. Section 92 of the Constitution Act, 1867 (formerly the British North America Act, 1867), places municipalities under provincial jurisdiction; therefore, provincial statutes can create or dissolve local governments.

Legislation Affecting Research   Under the common law in effect throughout Canada, except Quebec, the public has absolutely no legal access to local government information—that's right, *none*. But the good news is, with the introduction of hundreds of pieces of provincial and municipal legislation, a lot of information is now available.

It is not always a simple task to comprehend the laws that give us access to information. This area of law is chaotic and cumbersome, and even the courts are struggling to come to grips with it. Therefore, consider the following comments as *guidelines*, rather than rules, for doing research at this level of government.

The main piece of legislation that affects you as a researcher is the *Municipal Act* or its equivalent provincial statute. (In Ontario, however, the freedom-of-information law, Bill 34, legislates further legal access to local government information starting in 1991). The Municipal Act states in part that anything in the possession of the municipal clerk is public information. In addition, some local governments have passed by-laws specifying what information can be disposed of. Many special-purpose bodies abide by totally different rules, because they have been created by different provincial departments. (Special-purpose bodies are discussed in more detail on pages 104–106.)

Studying the pertinent legislation is not absolutely necessary, but if your research needs consistently involve municipal sources, it is worthwhile. For the occasional user it may be unnecessarily confusing. In Ontario, for instance, the Municipal Act states, with certain exceptions, that *records, books, documents,* and *accounts* in the possession of the clerk must be made available for public inspection. Other provinces have similar provisions. These terms, however, are open to a lot of interpretation; there has been legal wrangling over how generic a term like "record" or "document" is, and a few court cases have ensued. Also, the Ontario legislation doesn't explain that only *factual* information, such as minutes of council, by-laws, and resolutions, is public. Excluded are internal staff documents, such as municipal staff reports that might not be discussed in council or reports by local government solicitors.

Don't let this deter you. This chapter will show you that a lot of information can be retrieved without expert knowledge of the legislation. However, an understanding of the laws can help you if you are in that rare situation where you are being denied information.

INFORMATION AVAILABLE FROM LOCAL SOURCES

If you've never used your local government to obtain information, you may not be aware of what you're missing. Local governments, after all, are involved in virtually every area of your life and store an infinite range of information. Just ponder the tremendous scope of local government authority: municipal governments pave roads and remove the snow from them, collect and dispose of garbage, administer and often operate public transportation systems, provide police and fire protection, handle building and plumbing inspection, and provide a wide range of services, from day care to parks. Local government may also license over a hundred types of businesses. Its powers allow it to dictate how you can develop your property and how your neighbourhood can develop. These are only a few of its activities.

The kinds of information you can access are just as impressive. Much of it isn't available in published form but rather in records and files. The information you seek is kept on file for varying lengths of time and can be stored in any number of places in a municipality.

BEGINNING YOUR RESEARCH

Where do you begin your search for information? It is advisable to arm yourself with a rudimentary knowledge of the structure of your local government. This makes it far easier to find specific kinds of information. For instance, if you're searching for a health regulation and you know there is a health department, you won't waste your time approaching the building department. Some local governments publish organizational manuals listing departments and officials and their areas of authority. If there isn't one available in your area, you can write to the municipal clerk, asking for the name of the department that can best meet your needs.

A good, quick guide to understanding the types of local governments in your province is Volume Two of the *Corpus Almanac & Canadian Sourcebook*, found in your public library. In a page or two the editor unravels the local government structure of each province; included are the names and addresses of the municipal clerks.

The clerk is perhaps the most knowledgeable official in any local government. The clerk's powers, which are provided for in the provincial Municipal Acts, include recording the minutes of council and retaining the various kinds of information.

Begin by writing to the local clerk, outlining as precisely as possible what it is you wish to know. You might want to find out, for instance, how to apply for a business licence. I advise writing or telephoning, as opposed to showing up in person unannounced—it usually yields better results. If you visit a municipal department demanding information that could take the staff two solid days to obtain, you may be told the information is not available. This shouldn't come as a surprise. And don't interpret the denial as a case of government secrecy. Municipal governments, like other institutions, have been affected by budget cutbacks, and there is only so much their staff can accomplish. Keep this in mind, and your information search will proceed much more smoothly.

Telephoning the government is not always desirable, either, especially large municipal governments, because it can be difficult to reach the clerk. Putting your request in writing makes life easier for the staff. The clerk usually reroutes your letter to the correct department or replies with advice about where to find the information you need. By writing, you also minimize your chances of being denied information, because the staff has to put the denial in writing and state a reason. It's generally easier to honour your request.

I have singled out the clerk as a key employee. If, however, you are fortunate enough to live in a municipality with a local archives, you can also contact the archivist. He or she usually knows everything there is to know about the kinds of information available from the municipality and how to access them.

WHEN THE DOORS CLOSE

You may encounter a situation where a local government official refuses to allow you to inspect records. Sometimes this is the result of wording your request improperly. An example of a poorly worded request is: "Will you give me the name of the company that applied for the licence to run the dog kennel down the street?" The government official may not tell you because the Municipal Act and corresponding acts say that you may *inspect*, and obtain copies of, documents—nothing is mentioned about offering verbal information. This is a better way to get that information: "May I inspect the licence of the dog kennel down the street?" A request worded in this way also produces better results because in most municipalities the information is in the possession of the clerk, and the public, therefore, has the right to examine it.

Here's another example of an incorrect approach: you write to the clerk of the City of Toronto requesting copies of documents that show the election expenses of elected officials. The City of Toronto does not legally require local politicians to file this information, but most of them do. Some of these politicians have asked that the clerk's department not make copies of these documents freely available to the public. The correct approach is to ask to *inspect* the records. You would be allowed to do so, and you wouldn't be stopped if you wanted to photograph or make notes of them.

If you encounter a situation where you are flatly denied access to some information in the clerk's possession, ask the official to identify the provincial statute or regulations, or local government by-laws, prohibiting you from seeing the material. If the official cannot answer this question, point out that the Municipal Act (or equivalent provincial statute) states that certain kinds of information in the clerk's possession must be made available for public inspection. (But keep in mind that the information you seek may for some reason be exempt from this and other acts.)

If you are still denied access to a document or record that you feel you have a legal right to view, you can take your local government to County Court, requesting an order, called *mandamus*, to make the document available to you.

That's exactly what happened in April 1974 when a local resident and taxpayer took the City of Timmins to court because he had been denied certified copies of the municipal accounts. He argued that he was legally entitled to the invoices and vouchers because the Municipal Act stated that all information in possession of the clerk was public—and he won. Similar cases have resulted in other municipalities introducing freedom of information by-laws, detailing what the public is allowed to see.

There hasn't been a flood of these cases throughout Canada because most citizens don't use local governments as a source of information unless they are directly affected by an issue. Those who do often end their search unnecessarily when they're denied information. To repeat: if you're being denied information, take the matter a few steps further—chances are you will succeed. After all, like you, the government would rather avoid the messy business of litigation unless a grand principle is involved.

SPECIAL-PURPOSE BODIES

When you deal with special-purpose bodies, you may sometimes be unable to find statutes explaining what information you have a right to, and sometimes you may discover that a special-purpose body has an unwritten policy. The municipality's legal department can help clarify these policies.

For instance, I once wanted basic information on a few questionable Toronto companies. In Toronto, unlike most Canadian municipalities, a special-purpose body, the Metro Licensing Commission, regulates and licenses most Toronto businesses. It was set up by the Ontario government as a kind of consumer protection service, similar in function to the Better Business Bureau, and there are no statutory requirements compelling it to make information available to the public. I was told by the commission that I wouldn't be given any information, other than whether the companies held business licences and whether there were any complaints on file. I wouldn't be given any details of these complaints, nor would even basic information, such as the address of a company, be forthcoming. The employee at the commission insisted that I would be told nothing more unless I was an interested party involved in an accident or lawsuit.

The Metropolitan Toronto legal department, however, said otherwise. The lawyer in charge of handling decisions for the commission informed me that the commission has an unwritten policy by which the public can inspect a company's address, names of directors (if on file), and licence number. (The full application form for a business licence cannot be inspected, however, because it may contain information about a person's criminal record and the municipality could be sued for disclosing such information.) The public also has the right to inspect minutes of the commission's meetings and, possibly, the minutes of any special hearings dealing with applications for a licence under unusual circumstances. This was obviously far more information than the first government official had said was available to me.

DOCUMENTS AVAILABLE FOR PUBLIC INSPECTION

By this time you are probably interested in knowing exactly *what* information *is* available to the general public. As I have stressed throughout this chapter, this varies considerably from province to province and depends on how you conduct your information search. While you have a legal right to certain information in every province, some local governments give more than is legally required, and others don't give you the minimum amount of information you are entitled to unless you take the matter to court. The following are some of the kinds of records (out of potentially hundreds) that can usually be obtained and that have assisted me in my own research.

Council Minutes   Every municipality keeps minutes of its council meetings and makes them available to you on request. The quality of the minutes varies widely. In some cases the council of the municipality requests that the clerk keep full minutes, similar to those in *Hansard* (the transcript of the debates of the House of Commons). From such minutes you can learn how a decision evolved and what opinions were expressed by the council members. On the other hand, minutes may be very sketchy and contain little more than what decisions were made. Minutes are sometimes printed in both English and French.

A word of caution: if you are looking for resolutions or by-laws, keep in mind that an amendment to them may have been adopted at a later meeting. Also, check the appendix of the minutes for any documents or studies that were discussed at council meetings and that may be included.

Policy Decisions of Special-Purpose Bodies   Your local clerk can tell you which special-purpose bodies operate in your area. You may, for example, want to find out what a library board's policy is on shelving children's books. Or perhaps you want to know who is allowed to drive a taxi in your municipality. In many cases the meetings and minutes of a special-purpose body are open to the public.

School Support Lists   Most municipalities keep these computerized lists to keep track of who supports the public and separate school systems financially. The information is compiled by the provincial government and is organized alphabetically by surname. These lists can be highly useful if you want to trace someone. For example, I once wanted to find the home address of Gordon Lightfoot. Lightfoot is one of Canada's most popular entertainers and is naturally a private person with an unlisted telephone number. But the 1976 school support lists for the City of Toronto made it possible to find his address.

Practically everyone's name appears on school support lists. Other information the lists provide include all properties owned by those listed, whether they are Canadian citizens (or other British subject) or aliens, whether they live at the address shown, and whether they are the owner of the building or a tenant.

School support lists are kept in different departments, depending on the local government. The City of Toronto keeps them in its archives.

Tax Assessment Rolls   These are compiled by provincial governments for tax purposes, in this case to assess land taxes. They're generally arranged by address and indicate if the owner or tenant resides at the location; they also give the dimensions of the property. Older (pre-1970s) tax assessment rolls contain much more information, including a person's occupation, number of children, and if you go back to before the turn of the century, the number of cattle, dogs, and horses the person owned!

Voters' Lists   These are kept for each level of government. At the local level, they are arranged by street and compiled whenever there is a municipal election. They list who lives at an address, whether the person is married, and whether he or she is an owner or tenant. Voters' lists provide another method of tracing someone, provided, of course, you have some indication of which neighbourhood a person lives in.

Building Permit Records   You won't be able to look at the floor plans for a local bank, but you can probably inspect standard building permit applications that have been approved. Figure 13.1 shows such an application; you can see the typical kinds of information that must be filed, including the property owner's name, address, and telephone number. It's a handy source for tracing an elusive landlord!

Committee of Adjustment Records   These records are similar to building permits. The two-sided form, reproduced in Figure 13.2, must be completed by property owners who wish to be exempt from local by-laws when altering a building. They must provide their name, address, telephone number, and the names and addresses of any mortgagees.

Local Politicians' Files   In some municipalities local politicians (including, but not only, aldermen) may donate their files to the municipality once they retire. These files can provide a wealth of information on countless subjects. Most of it has been prepared by expert staff researchers, not necessarily by the local politicians themselves. Take advantage of this information.

Archives   As mentioned on page 103, some municipalities keep archives. If this is true of your local government, make an appointment to visit this department. The City of Toronto archives, one of the best in North America, has an extensive collection of records on every topic affecting Torontonians. This includes files donated by special-interest groups, photographs, maps, artifacts, and much more.

Figure 13.1   Sample Municipal Building Department Application

PERMIT APPLICATION

Please type or print

MUNICIPAL NUMBER (S)	PROPERTY ADDRESS

TYPE OF WORK

☐ Building   ☐ H.V.A.C.   ☐ Plumbing/Drainage   ☐ Exterior Signage   ☐ Demolition

EXISTING USE OF PROPERTY	NO. OF DWELLING UNITS

PROPOSED USE OF PROPERTY	NO. OF DWELLING UNITS

DESCRIPTION OF WORK

☐ Build   ☐ Interior Alterations   ☐ Additions   ☐ Change of Occupancy   ☐ Demolish   HUDAC NO. :|_|_|_|_|_|_|

Please give details _____

ESTIMATED COST OF PROPOSED WORK	NUMBER OF STOREYS		CONSTRUCTION TYPE
	ABOVE GRADE	BELOW GRADE	
$			☐ Combustible ☐ Non-Combustible

NAME OF OWNER	TELEPHONE
ADDRESS	
	(POSTAL CODE)

NAME OF APPLICANT	TELEPHONE
ADDRESS	
	(POSTAL CODE)

I, _____ , of the City of Toronto in the Municipality of Metropolitan Toronto, do solemnly declare:

1. That I am the owner / authorized agent of the owner named in the above application for a permit.
2. That the plans and specifications submitted are prepared for the work described in the permit application.
3. That the information supplied by me in the application and in the materials filed by me with the application is correct.
4. That the proper legal name(s) of the registered owner(s) of the property is/are:
   (strike out if applicant is authorized agent)

4. That to the best of my knowledge, information and belief the proper legal name(s) of the registered owner(s) of the property is/are:
   (strike out if applicant is owner)

And I make this Solemn Declaration conscientiously believing it to be true, and knowing it is of the same force and effect as if made under oath and by virtue of "The Canada Evidence Act".

Applicant's
Signature: _____

Declared before me at the City of Toronto in the Municipality of Metropolitan Toronto

this _____ day of _____ in the year 19 _____.

A Notary Public Commissioner, etc. _____

My Commission expires on: _____

Figure 13.2   Sample Application for Exemption from a Municipal By-law

APPLICATION FOR MINOR VARIANCE OR FOR PERMISSION

The undersigned hereby applies to the Committee of Adjustment for the City of Toronto under section 44 of The Planning Act, 1983, for relief, as described in this application, from By-law No. _____ .

1   Name of Owner:

2   Address: Postal Code:

    Telephone   (home):   (business):

3   Name of Agent (if any):

4   Address: Postal Code:

    Telephone   (home):   (business):

5   Names and addresses of any mortgagees, holders of charges or other encumbrancers, please include postal code:

6   Nature and extent of relief applied for:

7   Why is it not possible to comply with the provisions of the By-law?

8   Legal description of subject lands (registered plan number and lot number or other legal description and, where applicable, street and number):

9   Dimensions of lands affected:

    Frontage: Depth: Area: Width of Street:

10 Particulars of all buildings on or proposed for the subject lands, (specify ground floor area, gross floor area, number of storeys, width, length, height, etc.):

    Existing: _____

    Proposed: _____

Figure 13.2   *continued*

11   Location of all buildings and structures on or proposed for the subject lands, (specify distance from side, rear and front lot lines):

Existing: _____

Proposed: _____

12   Date of acquisition of subject lands:

13   Date of construction of all buildings and structures on subject lands: _____

14   Existing uses of the subject property: _____

15   Existing uses of abutting properties: _____

16   Length of time the existing uses of the subject property have continued:

17   Municipal services available (check appropriate box(es):

☐ Water   ☐ Connected   ☐ Sanitary Sewers   ☐ Connected   ☐ Storm Sewers

18   Present Official Plan provisions applying to the land: _____

19   Present Restricted Area By-law (Zoning By-law) provisions applying to the land: _____

20   Has the owner previously applied for relief in respect of the subject property?   ☐ Yes   ☐ No
If the answer is "yes," describe briefly:

_____

_____

_____

21   Is the subject property the subject of a current application for consent under section 49   ☐ Yes   ☐ No
of the Planning Act?

Signature of Applicant or Authorized Agent

Dated at the _____ *of* _____ *this* _____ *day of* _____ *19* ____

I, _____ *of the* _____ *of* _____

in the _____ *of* _____

solemnly declare that: All of the above statements are true, and I make this solemn declaration conscientiously believing it to be true and knowing that it is of the same force and effect as if made under oath.

Declared before me at the

_____ *of* _____

in the
      Judicial District of

_____ *this* _____

day of _____ *A.D. 19* _____

_____

A Commissioner, etc.

Records of Back Taxes and Work Orders   This kind of information is much more difficult for the public to obtain. For example, land taxes owed on a property or violations of city by-laws are two kinds of information that are generally available only to a lawyer acting for a prospective home buyer. However, it may be valuable enough to you that you hire a lawyer to obtain it for you.

Water Bills   You may be able to find out if a homeowner has paid his or her water bill. This information, which can indicate a person's financial stability, can sometimes be obtained verbally from the Water Revenue Branch or equivalent department.

Accessing Provincial Government Sources

Do you want to gather information on a private company to prepare yourself for a job interview? Are you making a loan and need information on the financial stability of either an individual or a company? Are you hiring a chauffeur and would like to examine an applicant's driver's record? Do you need a reliable source to verify someone's marital status, change of name, or death?

You can answer all of these queries using provincial government sources, but it requires sophisticated digging. You may have to study this chapter patiently more than once. In many cases you can obtain this information for under $10.

Provincial governments have a broad mandate. A partial list of their responsibilities includes taxation (as it relates to the provinces), the administering of prisons, natural resources, property, civil rights, marriages, and divorces. A comprehensive list of provincial jurisdictions is found in Section 92 of the Constitution Act, 1867. One thing you can count on: there is a wealth of publicly available information on people and business at this level of government.

Provincial governments are arranged in a myriad of ministries, departments, agencies, boards, commissions, and Crown corporations, each of which has its own structure and functions.

LOCATING DEPARTMENTS AND CIVIL SERVANTS

The quickest way to locate the most useful body and civil servant for your purposes is to telephone the provincial *hotline* in your area. The staffs operating these hotlines, or general inquiry numbers, are trained to refer you to the appropriate place—quickly. The hotline numbers are

- Yukon Territory: (403) 667-5431

- Northwest Territories: (403) 873-2611

- British Columbia: (604) 387-1337

- Alberta: (403) 427-4366

- Saskatchewan: (306) 787-6291

- Manitoba: (204) 945-3744

- Ontario: (416) 965-3535

- Quebec: (418) 643-7366

- New Brunswick: 1-800-442-4400 or (506) 453-2240

- Nova Scotia: (902) 424-2700

- Prince Edward Island: (902) 737-3612

- Newfoundland: (709) 737-3610.

These inquiry numbers are handy if you don't know where to start. Be patient: you may have to speak to two or three parties before you reach the civil servant who can help you. If you plan to use provincial government sources on a regular basis, however, familiarize yourself with the directories that help you pinpoint the correct provincial body and, equally important, the most knowledgeable civil servant. The directories discussed below are also used by hotline staff.

Every provincial government has a publisher—often called the Queen's Printer—who distributes provincial publications, such as provincial telephone directories. These directories can be especially helpful. They are generally divided into an alphabetical listing of all the provincial civil servants—from secretaries to cabinet ministers—and a listing of the various bureaucratic bodies, with civil servants listed according to title. Usually a brief description of the responsibilities of the body and a general inquiry number are given.

Some provinces also publish a handy complementary volume to the telephone directory that lists key words that refer you to the appropriate body. For example, if you need to find a contact for provincial grants, you would search under the key word "grants." These directories have different names. In Ontario, for example, it's called the *Kwic Index*.

Similar, privately-published directories can be equally useful. These include the *Corpus Almanac & Canadian Sourcebook* and *The Corpus Administrative Index* (published quarterly). These directories, usually available in any library, can be used for many different purposes. For example, if you want to know the telephone number of the provincial government publisher, search under "Queen's Printer." (The only exception is Alberta, where it is listed under "The Public Affairs Bureau.") The *Canadian Almanac and Directory* provides information similar to that found in the Corpus publications.

LOCATING PROVINCIAL GOVERNMENT PUBLICATIONS

A wealth of thoroughly researched material has been assembled for provincial governments by knowledgeable civil servants, hired consultants, private research firms, university project groups, and so on—you just have to know where to find it. Several reference sources can help you, and they are described in the following pages.

Microlog Index   The best reference source is the *Microlog Index*. This is a monthly and annual index published by Micromedia Limited, Toronto, and most public libraries subscribe to it. For the index every government publication from every level of government is scrutinized for material with research value; selected material is then microfilmed and indexed.

Micromedia sells the microfilm reports and studies for a fee. Before you pay a fee, check through the *Microlog Index* in your nearest library, list the materials you want, then find out if they are kept in your library or are easily available from the ministry that produced them or from the government bookstore. If not, write to Micromedia Limited, Document Delivery Services, Technical Information Centre, 165 Hotel de Ville, Place du Portage Phase II, Hull, Quebec J8X 3X2, or telephone 1-800-567-9669 (in Ontario, Quebec, or Atlantic Canada), (819) 770-9928, or FAX (819) 770-9265. The cost of paper reports varies depending on the volume. A report with 200–300 pages would cost $40 while a 50-page report costs $15. Microfiche copies are considerably less expensive.

If you can't find the information you're looking for in the *Microlog Index*, try the other routes described below; they are also used by the Microlog staff, but there is always the chance that something has been omitted.

Bibliographic Checklist   Almost every provincial government publishes a bibliographic checklist of material produced by its different bodies. These include official reports, administrative reports, statistical reports, periodicals, special reports, catalogues, and bibliographies. Most material published by a provincial government is included in these checklists.

The following is a list of the bibliographic checklists for all provinces and territories, except the Yukon Territory and Newfoundland, which were undergoing changes when this list was being assembled. While some of the following titles may change, you can easily find any new names by calling the legislative library of each province:

- The Northwest Territories' *Publications Catalogue* (annual)

- *British Columbia Government Publications Monthly Checklist*

- Alberta's *Publications Catalogue* (quarterly and annual)

- *Manitoba Government Publications Monthly Checklist*

- *Checklist of Saskatchewan Government Publications* (monthly)

- *Liste mensuelle des publications du gouvernement du Québec* (monthly) and *Liste mensuelle des publications du gouvernement du Québec index des titres de l'année* (annual)

- *Ontario Government Publications Monthly Checklist* and *Ontario Government Publications Annual Catalogue*

- *New Brunswick Government Publications Quarterly List* and *New Brunswick Government Documents* (annual)

- *Publications of the Province of Nova Scotia Monthly Checklist* and *Publications of the Province of Nova Scotia* (annual)

- *Prince Edward Island Government Publications Checklist* (monthly)

These lists include most of the material published at the provincial government level. The remainder of the material is more difficult to locate and is found in other places.

Departmental Lists   Departmental or ministry lists are bibliographies of published materials, quite independent of the checklists previously discussed. These titles may or may not appear on the main checklists. To learn about departmental lists, contact the library of the department concerned and ask to speak with its librarian, or contact the department's communications officer.

Other Lists   Some departments or bodies print lists of all the material they publish. These lists are more up-to-date than the regular provincial checklists—an item may appear on this list three months before appearing on the checklist. Having your name added to the mailing list for this information is not always easy. You should be able to offer a valid reason; for example, perhaps you're involved in a business venture that falls under a particular department. Start by contacting either the departmental library or its publicity co-ordinator (sometimes called a communications officer).

Limited Distribution Reports   There are also publications, known as *limited distribution reports*, that aren't included on any type of checklist. These reports or studies are often highly technical or of limited public interest and are classified as limited distribution reports for a number of reasons: the department may think there isn't enough demand to warrant a large print run; the department may want to save money and, by classifying the reports as such, it is not required to translate them into French. In other words, the government doesn't label the material in this fashion to hide it but to save money. To learn about these reports, contact the library of the department concerned, or the communications officer or publications co-ordinator.

Canadian News Index   Most studies or reports, however they are classified, are mentioned in the media. Thus, you can use the *Canadian News Index* at your nearest library as a guide, searching under your subject.

Other Provincial Government Business   If you want to supplement the media coverage of the work of provincial governments, there is a variety of sources at your fingertips. For example, legislative minutes are available at most libraries. Libraries also keep copies of the *Provincial Legislative Record*, published by CCH Canadian Ltd. This newsletter appears twenty times a year and lists government bills that are introduced. The *Public Sector*, published by Southam Communications Ltd., is a weekly newsletter providing analyses of federal and provincial policies, pending legislation, and new laws. It provides a quarterly reference index. *Canadian News Facts* can also be helpful. Published bi-weekly, it provides a synopsis of important news, including information relating to all levels of government. It is indexed quarterly and annually and is kept at most libraries. *Canadian News Facts* is a good source for dates and events, while *Provincial Legislative Record* and legislative minutes are excellent sources for probing further.

The remainder of this chapter is devoted to key sources of information that are pertinent for gathering data on *people* and *businesses*. They also indicate the scope of information available at this level of government. There are, of course, countless other sources from a vast number of provincial government bodies—enough to fill a book on their own.

If you require sources that are not discussed in the following pages, telephone your provincial government hotline for assistance, search for leads through the directories mentioned, or contact the communications department of the ministry or department involved.

BUSINESS RECORDS

Many kinds of provincial government records give insights into the corporate structure and financial stability of companies. Most of the information is available to the public from the provincial Ministry of Consumer and Commercial Relations or its equivalent department.

When you conduct a company search, keep in mind the three types of businesses in Canada: sole proprietorships (provincially registered, usually owned and operated by a single individual), partnerships (provincially registered and owned by at least two individuals or companies), and corporations (provincially or federally incorporated and either private or public).

The kinds of information that you can find on each type of business varies considerably from province to province. In some provinces you can conduct a few straightforward searches in a single office and gather all the information you need. But in another province you may have to visit several offices and wade through a variety of different legal documents before you find what you want.

To find out how your provincial department operates, get in touch with the provincial registrar. Ask that official what kinds of business searches are possible in the province and where the information can be obtained. The following is a list of addresses of the provincial registrars across Canada; most of the business searches described later in this chapter can be done directly at these offices:

Yukon Territory
Territorial Secretary and Registrar General
P.O. Box 2703
Government of the Yukon Territory
Whitehorse, Yukon
Y1A 2C6
Telephone: (403) 667-5442
Telex: 036-8260

Northwest Territories
Registrar of Companies
Legal Registry
Department of Justice and Public Services
Government of the Northwest Territories
Yellowknife, Northwest Territories
X1A 2L9
Telephone: (403) 873-7492
Telex: 034-45528

British Columbia
Ministry of Finance and Corporate Relations
Corporate and Central Registry
2nd Floor, The Waddington Building
940 Blanshard Street
Victoria, British Columbia
V8W 3E6
Telephone: (604) 387-5101
Telex: 049-7351

Alberta
Registrar of Corporations
Alberta Consumer and Corporate Affairs
10365-97 Street
Edmonton, Alberta
T5J 3W7
Telephone: (403) 427-0430
Telex: 037-41848
TWX 610-831-1942
Facsimile (403) 422-1091

Saskatchewan
Corporations Branch
Saskatchewan Consumer and Commercial Affairs
1871 Smith Street
Regina, Saskatchewan
S4P 2N5
Telephone: (306) 787-2962

Manitoba
Consumer and Corporate Affairs
10th Floor
405 Broadway Avenue
1010 Woodsworth Building
Winnipeg, Manitoba
R3C 3L6
Telephone: (204) 945-2500

Ontario
Companies Branch
Ministry of Consumer and Commercial Relations
393 University Avenue, 2nd Floor
Toronto, Ontario
M5G 1E6
Telephone: (416) 596-3745

Quebec
Direction des entreprises
L'Inspecteur général des institutions financières
800, place D'Youville
6e étage
Québec, Québec
G1R 4Y5
Telephone: (418) 643-3625
Telex: 051-3706

Quebec (Montreal office)
Direction des entreprises
L'Inspecteur général des institutions financières
800, place Victoria
42e étage, Bureau 4208
Case Postale 246
Montréal, Québec 246
H4Z 1G3
Telephone: (514) 873-5324

New Brunswick
Department of Justice
Corporate and Trust Affairs
P.O. Box 6000, Centennial Building
Fredericton, New Brunswick
E3B 5H1
Telephone: (506) 453-2703
Telex: 014-46230

Nova Scotia
Registrar of Joint Stock Companies
Department of the Attorney General
1660 Hollis Street
P.O. Box 1529
Halifax, Nova Scotia
B3J 2Y4
Telephone: (902) 424-7770
Telex: 019-22884

Prince Edward Island
Corporations Division
Department of Justice
P.O. Box 2000, Shaw Building
Charlottetown, Prince Edward Island
C1A 7N8
Telephone: (902) 892-5411
Telex: 014-44154

Newfoundland
Registry of Deeds, Companies and Securities
Department of Justice
P.O. Box 4750
Confederation Building
St. John's, Newfoundland
A1C 5T7
Telephone: (709) 576-2591

A list of the general types of business searches that can be done are discussed in the next few pages. Because the laws governing businesses in each province are different, you will encounter different types of legal documents that must be filed with the provincial government and different names for the departments that handle this information.

The contents of the searches are *for the most part* the same across Canada, but the form the information takes varies considerably from province to province; therefore, these descriptions cannot be applied identically everywhere. They represent the basic kinds of searches for most provinces. Contact your provincial registrar for further details. Of course, these searches represent *provincial* sources only. There are also federal and court records, and these are discussed in Chapters 15 and 16.

A provincial business search, as I mentioned, can usually be conducted at the office of the registrar. It can take from a few hours to several days to conduct one search, depending on the complexity of the company records and the workload of the staff who handle public queries. Some provinces allow the public to place their requests by telephone and then pick up the information when it is ready. A small fee (usually under $5) is charged for most searches, excluding photocopying fees; in most provinces you can set up an account if you plan to do business searches on a regular basis.

Securities Commission Records   Compiling information about public companies is in many ways easier than about private companies. Public companies in Canada are those that raise capital by offering shares to the public. These shares are generally issued by companies through securities underwriters and are in turn sold to the public. Shares are often listed later on stock exchanges. In Canada stock exchanges are found in Toronto, Montreal, Winnipeg, Alberta, and Vancouver.

Public companies are governed by various provincial securities statutes and must make available to the public certain kinds of information to protect their shareholders. This information includes a prospectus (explaining how the company is structured and what it does); any press releases; regular, audited financial statements; *insider reports* (listing any insider shareholders—those who own 10 percent or more of a company—and any director or officer who owns shares); annual reports; debt structure (which reveals the company's borrowing habits and what assets are tied up by a secured loan); and a list of subsidiary companies. There are other filing requirements as well. You may request a complete list of all the documents that companies are required to file by asking the communications department of the Securities Commission in your area. The actual documents can be obtained at the government offices listed on pages 118–120. (In Ontario, however, OSC records are handled through Micromedia Ltd., 158 Pearl Street, Toronto, Ontario, M5H 1L3. Telephone: (416) 593-5211.)

If the company sells public shares in the United States, it must file even more detailed information with the U.S. Securities and Exchange Commission (SEC). Some of the SEC information may also be included in provincial securities commission files. You may find, for instance, Form 10-K, which is a detailed annual report made by a company giving information on such things as its products and services, markets, a list of its properties, any pending legal proceedings, five-year financial data, and sometimes the salaries of its directors and officers. A SEC Form 10-Q may also be included in provincial records. It provides an updated financial outlook since the previous Form 10-K was filed.

If you are researching a major public company, chances are that its shares are listed on a stock exchange. If so, you can probably inspect the documents discussed above at the stock exchange itself, free of charge. If you're not sure which public company is listed on what stock exchange, check a major daily newspaper in your area. The financial pages list all the stock exchanges and what companies trade on them. You then know what province to refer to.

You may, however, require information on a public company that is not listed on a stock exchange. Stocks of such companies are traded on an "unlisted market" (or "over the counter"). To research such companies, as well as companies that are listed on stock exchanges, you can do provincial securities commission searches. To do so, as for most searches, you must generally fill out a simple form listing the names of the companies and the documents you require. In some provinces, such as Ontario, you can find indexes to the documents that have been filed. The fee for requesting a particular document varies from province to province. In some large cities, the major public library will keep security commission records. For example, at the Metropolitan Toronto Library, you can view all OSC records free of charge and make copies at a fraction of the cost you would pay through the provincial Security Commission. Although information at libraries is not as up-to-date as it is at securities commissions, it is still up to date enough for most purposes.

There is an exception to the fees charged by various provincial securities commissions. In Quebec, you can view all of the documents free of charge, or be given the information over the telephone, also free of charge.

Corporate Search You can gather various kinds of basic information on any provincially registered corporation—as well as corporations registered in other provinces and federally registered corporations doing business in that province—by doing a corporate search. A straight corporate search provides such information as the correct name of the corporation and any *style* or *trade names* it uses for conducting business with the public, a list of directors and officers of the company, their addresses, any registered changes in this information, the date of incorporation, in many instances the structure of the corporation, and if and how shares are offered.

In some provinces, such as Nova Scotia and Ontario, a corporate search gives you only skeletal information on a business. On the other hand, a corporate search in British Columbia provides considerably more, including information on *encumbrances*. These include various kinds of debentures and can help determine the indebtedness or borrowing habits of a company. Encumbrances are detailed enough to show you what personal property assets (equipment and anything other than land or buildings) are tied up in a loan.

In Quebec, a corporate search will provide you with all of the information provided in an "Annual Return," which is a form all firms carrying on business in Quebec must fill out. The information includes such data as the location of the company's head office, the kind of business undertaken, the date and place of incorporation, the firm's total amount of debt in bonds and debentures, the date of the last annual meeting, the number of employees, where the company's real estate holdings are in Quebec, details of the capital stock of public companies, including a list of shareholders holding ten percent or more of the voting shares, information as to whether the firm is a public or private company, and identification of directors and officers.

Most provinces require you to fill out a form listing the corporate name and provincial corporation number of the corporation you're researching. You can find this number without charge by using the microfiche reader in the provincial office and scanning the set of microfiche that is usually kept beside the reader. These fiche contain an alphabetical list of all corporations registered in that province, including any corporations registered in another province that have an "extra-provincial" licence to operate in the province and any federally-registered corporations conducting business there. The fiche list the corporate name and date of incorporation.

If you can't find the name, it may be that the business is federally incorporated and not operating in that province; or it may be a provincially registered sole proprietorship or partnership; or it could be using another name. It is also possible, in a rare instance, that the name you are searching for has not yet been included in the fiche. To be certain, request the information without providing a corporation number. Some provinces provide you with a corporate search file even if you don't include the corporate number. The number is used to speed up your request.

Corporate searches vary in cost, although the fees are generally nominal. There's no charge in Quebec, and it is one of the only provinces to offer a corporate search to anyone over the telephone.

Business Style Search   A *style* or *trade name* is the name a company uses to carry on business with the public. Sometimes a corporation uses one name for the public and another for government filings.

To do a business style search, simply fill out a form at the provincial office, providing the style name. You receive a photocopy of the style registration card, which gives the name of the corporation, and then you have to follow this up with a corporate search. A corporate search provides you with a list of all the style names the business is using. If you don't have the corporate name, but do have the style name, you must do a business style search first.

There is a time frame in which the registration of style names remains valid. If a business doesn't apply to renew the registration of its style name, the previous application form is removed from the file and sent into storage—in some provinces into the provincial archives. You must then apply to the archives to obtain the information.

Sole Proprietorship Search   A sole proprietorship search provides the name and address of the sole proprietor, the nature of the business, and when it began.

To do a sole proprietorship search in most provinces, you fill out a form providing the name of the business. In Quebec, the procedure is different, because it is governed by civil law instead of English common law, like the rest of the provinces. In Quebec, the first step is to contact the Montreal or Quebec City office responsible for company records. A telephone call is sufficient to obtain the proper name of the sole proprietorship, the name and address of the owner, and the date the business was registered. For further details you must contact the local district court house where the firm was registered. Sometimes you can do this over the telephone. The local court house in that district can inform you of the marital status of the firm's owner, the name (and maiden name, if applicable) of the owner's spouse, where the couple was married, whether they are separated and, if divorced, which court granted the divorce and its writ number. (With the writ number you can go to the appropriate court and look up the divorce records, which would reveal any settlements.) The information also includes the owner's occupation, residential address, and the type of business carried on. If a style name is being used, this will also be included.

Partnership Search   The partnership search, also conducted at the provincial office responsible for business records, provides a list of business partners, their addresses, and the date of registration of the business. It may be that several corporations own the business, in which case you have to do a corporate search on each corporation.

Personal Property Security Act Search   Various provincial statutes, such as the Personal Security Act (PPSA), enable creditors to register security agreements involving personal property. (Real property, such as land and anything erected on the land, is registered at land registry offices. This is discussed later in this chapter.) The kinds of security agreements registered vary widely from province to province.

Ontario, Manitoba, Saskatchewan, and the Yukon each have a PPSA, and some of the other provinces are moving in this direction. PPSA offices keep a record of registered *financing statements* (which constitute *notice* of a security agreement) and related *financing change statements* involving personal property for *individuals* and *businesses*. These include various kinds of security agreements, such as chattel mortgages, conditional sales contracts, assignments of book debts, and bonds. Sometimes you come across a notice of a document labelled simply, "general security agreement."

All of these terms describe security agreements registered by creditors to protect their interests. They offer different terms, depending on the type of contract involved; what is common to all of them is that a creditor has some legal right to the assets of an individual or a business (excluding, as already noted, real property).

Because the PPSA is a *notice-filing* system, you cannot obtain a copy of the security agreement. However, if you are a debtor, an execution creditor, or have an interest in the collateral, you have a right to a copy of the security agreement or information concerning the amount of the indebtedness. To obtain it, you must send a request in writing to the secured party.

If you require information on security agreements registered in a province without a Personal Property Security Act, you have to search for this type of information under different legislation, such as an Assignment of Book Debts Act.

A P.P.S.A. search can reveal everything from small consumer transactions to sales on credit to large-scale corporate financing. It is, of course, also of considerable value to anyone purchasing personal property, for example, a car or a boat, because it registers any liens against this property. In effect it warns the buyer that the personal property in question has been used for collateral in a registered loan—that is, as a lien against personal property.

In the provinces that use a PPSA system you should inquire if a basic PPSA search will provide you with information for all liens against all personal property. It may be that you must conduct several searches to get all of the information. For example, at the time of writing, Ontario was introducing a new piece of legislation, the Repairs and Storeage Liens Act (RSLA) which covers liens against automobiles. This means that if you were looking for liens against a car, you would conduct an RSLA search in Ontario. For further liens against other personal property you would then conduct a separate PPSA search.

PPSA searches can provide important clues as to a person's or company's borrowing habits. As stated, it may not specify the amount of indebtedness but generally gives you the lendor's name and address and sometimes detailed information about the purpose of the loan. Private investigators and skillful interviewers will follow up on these leads and interview the lendor. Obviously, it's unlikely that anyone who is not involved with the loan will be given access to confidential files, but careful questions can still reveal a good deal of specific information. There are, of course, no guarantees for what information you can get. It really depends on the skill of the interviewer and the reasons given for wanting the information. If, for example, the researcher is screening a company for a client who plans to invest in the company, carefully worded questions may reveal the approximate amount of the loan, part of the company's business plans, and possibly any new directions the company plans to take. With this kind of information the researcher is now in a better position to judge an individual's or company's overall indebtedness.

Corporations Securities Registration Act Search   In provinces that have both a Personal Property Securities Registration Act and a Corporations Registrations Securities Act (CSRA), the information you can obtain overlaps. The PPSA gives a brief description of the security agreement, whereas under the CSRA you can pull the actual *instrument* (the legal document that has created a right). The CSRA registers only *corporate* securities, not individual indebtedness.

In some provinces you may have to go to several departments and find the information under several statutes in order to determine the indebtedness of a corporation. In Nova Scotia, for example, you must do a CSRA search and then look under the Registry of Deeds.

On the other hand, in Ontario the situation has been simplified with legislative changes. At the time of this writing Ontario was planning to abolish its CSRA and amalgamate the information under a newly revised computerized PPSA system. This will mean that a PPSA search would allow a researcher access to the same information and getting at that information will be much easier.

With the exception of the basic corporate search, the kinds of searches described in this chapter apply to provinces other than Quebec. Because of its civil law system, Quebec doesn't have a PPSA, CSRA, or any other similar filing system. Still, it is possible to conduct various searches which will indicate some of a company's debt structure. (Note, however, that not all debt is legally required to be filed.) Among the documents you should look for are: *Nantissements* (commercial pledges), *Hypothèques* (mortgages), *Actes de Fiducie* (trust deeds), and *Loi sur Cessions de Bien en Stock* (assigning inventory).

To locate these records you must first find the head office address of the company. This you can find through either of the two Quebec offices listed on page 119. With the address you can pinpoint the judicial district that covers the location of the company. The records are kept in the local court house in a department sometimes known as the "Registration Bureau."

The documents in question do not necessarily disclose the amount of the debts, although specific amounts may be recorded. Often you will learn which financial institutions are putting up the money. This, of course, is one step towards understanding how much debt is involved and what its purpose is. Again, private investigators and researchers will use the address of the money lender as a lead and then interview a bank manager or loans officer.

These documents will often list the collateral a company has used for a loan or bond issue. The list can sometimes reveal a company's entire inventory and equipment if these have been used as collateral.

The searches at court houses can be confusing. It may save you time and money to hire a professional title searcher to pull specific documents. Locating a freelance title searcher is easier if you go directly to the court house. Generally, you will find many such researchers busy at work there, and many of them are willing to take on additional work. The most experienced researchers in this field are often notaries, since it is this professional body that files the documents. To locate a list of notaries who work in the area in which you are examining documents, you can contact their professional association, the Chambre des Notaries du Québec, 630 Ouest Blvd., Dorchester, Montréal, Québec, H3B 1T6, or call the association directly at (514) 879-1793.

The cost of conducting searches involving company debt in Quebec are more expensive than in other provinces. Some court houses charge an hourly rate for allowing you to research files as well as a hefty photocopying charge.

Certificate of Status Search   A Certificate of Status search varies in cost, depending on whether you want a verbal reply or a certified document. Most provincial offices can tell you if a business has been dissolved or if it has made all the filings required under provincial law that would give it a valid certificate of status. The name of this document differs slightly from one province to another.

Corporations Tax Branch Search   In some provinces the
Ministry of Revenue or corresponding department can tell you
if a business has filed up-to-date tax returns. If it hasn't, the
company may be in financial trouble.

Workers' Compensation Board Records   By contacting
your provincial Workers' Compensation Board, you may be
able to find out if a business is in good standing with the
department.

LAND REGISTRY FILES

Are you thinking of purchasing a house, and you want to find
out how much the current owners paid for it? Do you want to
trace the land ownership and research any liens and mortgages
against a property? You're researching a company and want to
see if it has taken out a mortgage on any properties? Or
perhaps you want to know if the government has registered the
fact that you've paid off your mortgage? All such inquiries can
be answered by using provincial land registry files.

First, establish where the land is and which registry office is
applicable. You can obtain a list of land registry offices from
the Land Registrar in your province. The addresses and names
of these registrars can be found in the *Corpus Almanac & Canadian Sourcebook*, available in any library. The registrars can
also advise you how to proceed with your search.

In the following pages I offer some general guidelines on
how to search a title. These should *not* be construed as a fool-
proof method of title searching for the purpose of purchasing
land or a house. If you want to certify land ownership, hire a
lawyer; however, if it's information you want, a lot can be
obtained without the help of a lawyer.

A land registry office is a very busy place. At one time most
lawyers who specialized in real estate did their own title
searching. Today it is done by clerks, often on a piecemeal
basis for law firms and other professionals who require information on land ownership. These clerks, as well as the people
who run the offices, can be very helpful. Ask them how to
search the title of your property.

Legal Description   Begin by determining the legal description of the property you are searching. Properties are described

differently in each province; the terminology may vary even within a province. In Nova Scotia and Newfoundland they have a Book and Folio Number; in Alberta and British Columbia it is a Parcel Number; in Manitoba and Saskatchewan it is a Lot and Plan Number. And in Ontario you search for a Lot and Plan Number, a Lot and Concession Number, or a Parcel and Section Number.

Ask the Land Registrar or clerk at the Registry Office to see the assessment rolls; they will assist you in obtaining the correct legal description (which may require a visit to a separate office).

Land Registry   There are different systems in place for registering land ownership. You may, for example, encounter the centuries-old *Registry System*, which records land ownership in large books known as abstract books (or abstract indexes). These books contain summarized particulars of each instrument or legal document which affect the property you are searching. To inspect the abstract books, you fill out a form, sometimes known as a "request for service slip." You will be charged a fee to inspect the books. At the time of writing, the fee in Ontario, for example, was four dollars.

If the property you are searching has been split up or subdivided, you will likely have to inspect an extra abstract book for each subdivision.

Under the Registry System, you can trace land ownership back as far as you want. Lawyers generally trace ownership back forty years to ascertain the legal title of the property. The abstract books use the words, *deed* (or *grant*) and *mortgage*. A deed refers to a change in ownership; a mortgage indicates an encumbrance.

The information in the abstract book is recorded by hand and for this reason is not always up to date. To ensure you are inspecting the most recent information, you should check the Day Book or equivalent filing system.

If you want to inspect an original instrument, such as a mortgage, write down the instrument number from the abstract book. Ask for a "request for service slip" or its equivalent to process your request. Some of these documents include a Land Transfer Tax Affidavit, which states how much was paid for the property.

Occasionally, the purchase price is deliberately left out of the affidavit because the owner wishes to keep the information confidential. However, the owner pays property taxes to the provincial Ministry of Revenue, or equivalent Ministry, at a separate office. The property deed is stamped by the Ministry of Revenue and, subsequently, registered at the Registry Office. The receipt number for this transaction is kept at the Registry Office. Take down the receipt number and contact the Ministry—you may be able to learn the purchase price this way.

If you are trying to determine who owns a property, keep in mind that there are different forms of property ownership, meaning that more than one party owns a portion of the property; another type of split ownership is tenants in common. And, of course, one person may own property.

Property may also be owned by a company. If you want to find out who runs the company, you must first do a corporate search, described earlier in this chapter.

Land Titles   Another method of recording land ownership and the most modern of the two systems is the *Land Titles System*. Under this system, with certain exceptions, the provincial government *guarantees* the ownership of the property; this isn't the case under the Registry System. By completing a "request for service slip," or equivalent form, and paying a fee, you can access a register (or parcel register index) which contains a summary of the registered documents concerning the property you are searching. The fee in Ontario, for example, is four dollars.

The documents or instruments are labelled differently under the Land Titles System. A "mortgage" is known as a "charge," a "deed" is called a "transfer," and a "discharge" is referred to as a "cessation". Sometimes you can tell if a mortgage has been paid off if the word "charge" has been crossed off of the register.

You can access any instruments by filling out an additional form per document and paying a small fee. (In Ontario, however, there is no fee.)

The registry office also lists any liens against a property, such as a *Mechanic's Lien* (which in some provinces, such as Ontario, is called a *Contruction Lien*). If a tradesman has done some work on a property and hasn't been paid, he or she can register a Mechanic's Lien on the property at the registry office and then take legal action against the property owner.

As is the case under the Land Registry System, you should check the Day Book or its equivalent for the most up-to-date filings.

The procedures discussed for tracing land ownership generally apply in the province of Quebec. While the actual system of registration is different there than in the rest of the country, you can still pull deeds of sale and mortgages in the same manner. There are 82 land registration offices in Quebec which are often located in the local court house of the town or city closest to the land in question.

If, you run into any problems, remember that the Land Registrar, the clerks, and the freelance title searchers are generally very helpful.

MOTOR VEHICLES SEARCHES

Are you in a legal dispute and need a history of a driver's record? Or perhaps you are looking for an old friend, and city directories, tax assessment rolls, and voters' lists at every level of government have failed to give you any leads. In each of these instances, access to various provincial motor vehicle records may supply the information you need.

Accessibility of Information in Ontario   The public's right of access to such records varies widely from province to province. Ontario appears to be one of the most liberal provinces as far as right of access to this information is concerned. At the time of writing the first edition of this book, anyone could conduct a vehicle record search, driver record search, or accident report search in Ontario. The searches involve simply filling in a form. Now, however, the application form requires a "valid reason" for requesting this information. The staff are very liberal in determining which reasons are valid and will rarely turn down a request for this information.

To conduct a *motor vehicle search* in Ontario, you need the licence plate number of the car you want to research and/or a full name and address. This verifies the name and address of the plate's owner and the make of the car registered in that person's name. (By law, anyone taking up permanent residence in another province must file a change of address within three months.) The motor vehicle search also tells you the ownership of the plate for the current year and the previous three years. This search costs $5.

In Ontario you can conduct a *driver record search* with only a name, although not if the name is a common one, like Smith. Your chances of finding information are enhanced if you have other information that can identify the driver, such as date of birth, driver's licence number, or a middle initial.

This search tells you if the driver has had any convictions under Ontario's Highway Traffic Act or under the Criminal Code of Canada, with respect to driving a vehicle. To learn the actual details of these offences, you have to search through court records; they provide the date of any offences and a list of any suspensions. The cost is $5 per search.

As with other motor vehicle searches, to conduct an *accident report search*, you must fill out a form providing as much information as possible. In Ontario this type of search can be done by anyone, and a copy of a police accident report is provided. You should be able to give one party's name in full and the approximate date and place of the accident, or a driver's licence number. The cost is $10 per search.

Accessibility in Other Provinces   Other provinces record the same information provided in the above searches, but they are far more reluctant to release it. To do any of the above searches in the other provinces, you must submit a written request, giving a detailed explanation of why you are requesting the information and how you intend to use it. Each request is carefully monitored to respect individual privacy.

Yet this doesn't mean you can't obtain the information. In British Columbia, for example, if a company wants to hire a driver, it may be able to pull a driver's record if it can convince the provincial authorities that the data is being used for an employee check.

Here's a different kind of research request: if you want to trace a relative in Nova Scotia or Alberta and the government finds your request acceptable, it may contact the relative on your behalf and have them contact you.

To find out the policy in your province contact the Registrar of Motor Vehicles. (In some provinces the name varies slightly; for example, in British Columbia it is the Superintendent of Motor Vehicles.) Call the hotline number to reach this official.

PROVINCIAL VITAL STATISTICS OFFICES

There may be an occasion when you need to ascertain whether or not a person has married, had children, died, or changed his or her name. Each province keeps this information at its vital statistics office. Learning this information is not easy—access to it is usually determined on a *policy* basis. This means that each province reviews every request and decides whether the reasons given are valid. If, for example, you need information for a court proceeding, it may be provided. It may also be advantageous to have your lawyer request information for you, particularly if you require certified copies of documents rather than a verbal response.

Here is another example: you are a woman living with a man who you suspect is lying about his marital status. You may be able to learn the truth by putting your request in writing and stating your reason. In a case like this, the vital statistics office may tell you if the person has been married and the year of the marriage.

If you are a family member, you stand a better chance of obtaining copies of documents. If you are investigating someone else's background for a valid reason, you can probably obtain only verbal confirmation that an event occurred.

Put your request in writing, providing the reasons you want the information and how you intend to use it. Provide as much information about the person(s) as possible, including full name and approximate date of marriage or death. Fees vary but are generally nominal. The following is a list of provincial vital statistics offices and the names of those to whom you can make your inquiries:

Alberta
Mr. S. William Gilroy
Director
Division of Vital Statistics Alberta
Department of Community & Occupational Health
10130-112 Street
Edmonton, Alberta
T5K 2K4
Telephone: (403) 427-2681

British Columbia
Mr. Ron J. Danderfer
Director
Division of Vital Statistics
1515 Blanshard Street
Victoria, British Columbia
V8W 3C8
Telephone: (604) 387-0041

Manitoba
Ms. Margorie Kreton
Manitoba Community Services
Vital Statistics
254 Portage Avenue
Winnipeg, Manitoba
R3C 0B6
Telephone: (204) 945-3701

New Brunswick
Mrs. Marianne Wiezel
Registrar General
Vital Statistics Division
Department of Health
P.O. Box 6000
Fredericton, New Brunswick
E5B 5H1
Telephone: (506) 453-2385

Newfoundland
Mr. Norman M. Parker
Registrar General
Vital Statistics Division
Department of Health
St. John's, Newfoundland
A1C 5T7
Telephone: (709) 576-3308

Northwest Territories
Mrs. Vicki J. Hickey
Registrar General
Vital Statistics
Department of Justice and Public Services
Government of the Northwest Territories
Box 1320
Yellowknife, N.W.T.
X1A 2L9
Telephone: (403) 873-7404

Nova Scotia
Mr. D.F. Arthur
Deputy Registrar General
Department of Public Health

Halifax, Nova Scotia
B3J 2M9
Telephone: (902) 424-4374

Ontario
Mrs. D.H. Georgas
Deputy Registrar General
Macdonald Block
900 Bay Street
Toronto, Ontario
M7A 1Y5
Telephone: (416) 965-1687

Prince Edward Island
Ms. G.A. Melanson
Director
W.J.P. MacMillan Building
17 Haviland Street
P.O. Box 2000
Charlottetown, P.E.I.
C1A 7N8
Telephone: (902) 892-1001

Quebec
M. Lorenzo Servant
Responsable des Archives Civiles, Ministère de la Justice
Registre de référence
300 Boulevard Jean-Lesage
RC–20
Québec, Québec
G1K 8K6
Telephone: (418) 649-3527

Saskatchewan
Mr. Wilmer Berg
Director of Vital Statistics
T.C. Douglas Building
3475 Albert Street
Regina, Saskatchewan
S4S 6X6
Telephone: (306) 787-3092

Yukon Territory
Mrs. Arleen Kovac
Deputy Registrar General
Department of Health and Human Resources
Box 2703
Whitehorse, Yukon
Y1A 2C6
Telephone: (403) 667-5811

PROVINCIAL FREEDOM OF INFORMATION LAWS

Provincial freedom of information laws are a good means of finding out what sort of information the government keeps about you and whether it is accurate. You get a sense of just how much information provinces gather by reading Manitoba's access registry, *The Access to the Freedom of Information Act*, a 700-page book itemizing *every* record that province keeps on its citizens.

Most provinces are now moving to enact freedom of information laws. These laws have different names, but the principle involved in each of them is the same: that citizens have the legal right to see government information about themselves.

Manitoba, New Brunswick, Nova Scotia (which in 1977 became the first province to offer such legislation), Newfoundland, Ontario, and Quebec have proclaimed freedom of information laws. At the time of this writing, most of the other provinces were at various stages of enacting such legislation.

This legislation allows you to access many government files with information on you. But it also lists many exceptions, including denial of access to information that may hinder any investigatory proceeding and any that may invade another's privacy.

If the information you seek is denied, you can appeal. The appeal process varies considerably from province to province. For example, in Nova Scotia there is no provision to appeal a denial of information in the courts. But in New Brunswick you can refer the matter either to the provincial ombudsman or to a judge of the Supreme Court. In Manitoba you can appeal first to the provincial ombudsman and, if that fails, to the Court of Queen's Bench. In Ontario, you can appeal to the Information

Commissioner, who has incredible powers. (Unlike any other appeal mechanism, the Ontario commissioner has the final say —even having the power to overrule a cabinet minister's decision!)

The actual mechanics of retrieving personal information under freedom of information legislation also varies. To find out if there is a bill in effect in your province and what it provides, contact the government bookstore or visit the government section of your local library. You can also contact the department responsible for administering the law. If all of these leads fail, call the provincial hotline number given at the beginning of this chapter.

If there is no freedom of information law in effect in your province, you may still have access to information the government has about you. To learn what information this is, contact the individual or department involved in drafting any pending freedom of information legislation.

Accessing Federal Government Sources

With more than half a million employees on its payroll, the Government of Canada is the country's largest custodian of information. Many civil servants with expertise in virtually every field are available to help you with your information needs. Take advantage of their knowledge—after all, as a taxpayer, you're paying for it!

The jurisdictions of the federal government are broad. Set out in Section 91 of the Constitution Act, 1867, they cover everything from unemployment insurance to defence.

There are two fundamental divisions within the federal government: *departments* (including ministries and Crown corporations, all of which are structured differently and have various functions) and *commissions*, *boards*, and *councils* (independent of departments). Most of our information needs are supplied by departments.

LOCATING DEPARTMENTS AND CIVIL SERVANTS

The challenge of finding federal government sources is zeroing in on the appropriate department and, eventually, the most knowledgeable civil servant. To help you, the federal government has established a nationwide toll-free, bilingual referral service—Reference Canada. Operating under the jurisdiction of the Department of Supply and Services, Reference Canada staff direct you to the federal office that can best answer your enquiries.

In some instances, Reference Canada operates in conjunction with a provincial or territorial inquiry service. In these instances the name of the provincial/territorial service is used.

Reference Canada staff can help you obtain copies of reports, explain your eligibility for a grant, or refer you to the most suitable civil servant. Be patient if you don't find the right person immediately—it may take a few conversations. The following is a list of Reference Canada Service Bureaus, including their local and toll-free telephone numbers:

Yukon Territory
Yukon Inquiry Service
Telephone: In Whitehorse: 667-5811
              In other parts of the territory (toll-free):
              1-667-5955

British Columbia
Reference Canada
Telephone: In Vancouver: 666-5555
              In other parts of the territory (toll-free):
              1-800-663-1381
              Zenith 08918 (Atlin only)

Alberta
Reference Canada
Telephone: In Edmonton: 495-2021
              In Calgary: 292-4998
              In other parts of the province (toll-free):
              1-800-232-9481
              Telecommunication Device for the Deaf (TDD)
              Edmonton: 495-4161

Saskatchewan
Reference Canada
Telephone: In Regina: 780-6683
              In other parts of the province (toll-free):
              1-800-667-7160

Manitoba
Citizens' Inquiry Service
Telephone: In Winnipeg: 945-3744
In other parts of the province (toll-free):
1-800-282-8060
Telecommunication Device for the Deaf (TDD)
Winnipeg: 945-4796

Ontario
Reference Canada
Telephone: In Ottawa: 995-7151
In North Bay: 476-4910
In Toronto: 973-1993
In the Ottawa/Hull area (toll-free)
1-800-267-0340
In area codes 807 and 705 (toll-free)
1-800-461-1664
In other parts of the province (toll-free)
1-800-387-0700
Telecommunication Device for the Deaf (TDD)
Toronto: 973-8099

Quebec
Communication-Québec
Telephone: For local calls consult your telephone directory,
blue pages section under Communication—
Québec
For a toll-free long distance call, dial "0" and ask
for Zenith Communication-Québec

New Brunswick
New Brunswick Information Service
Telephone: In Fredericton: 453-2525
In other parts of the province (toll-free):
1-800-442-4400

Nova Scotia
Reference Canada
Telephone: In Halifax: 426-8092
In other parts of the province (toll-free):
1-426-8092

Prince Edward Island
Island Inquiries
Telephone: In Charlottetown: 368-5050
            In other parts of the province (toll-free):
            1-368-5050

Newfoundland
Reference Canada
Telephone: In St. John's: 772-4365
            In other parts of the province (toll-free):
            1-800-563-2432

An excellent reference source, and one the staff at Reference Canada use themselves, is the *Index to Federal Programs and Services*. This annual reference book, which is available at most libraries, lists approximately 1200 federal programs and services with brief descriptions of each; approximately 4500 addresses; regular and toll-free telephone numbers of many departments, and a subject index. If you plan to use federal government sources on a regular basis, it's worth purchasing a copy of this book from any bookstore associated with the Canadian Government Publishing Centre. (These bookstores are discussed later in this chapter.)

The federal government publishes detailed telephone directories for every province, including one for the Ottawa region. In addition, Southam Communications publishes the very useful *Corpus Administrative Index*. With a separate supplementary subject guide, it lists all federal and provincial government departments, key personnel, addresses, and telephone numbers. There are other Corpus books which elaborate on who is who in government. Similar directories include the *Corpus Almanac & Canadian Sourcebook* and the *Canadian Almanac & Directory*. These can all be found in most libraries.

LOCATING FEDERAL GOVERNMENT PUBLICATIONS

The following are various ways in which you can search for a federal government publication:

- You can telephone Reference Canada for assistance.

- You can search through the *Microlog Index* at the public library. (For a description of this index, refer to Chapter 12, "Using

Libraries in Canada," and Chapter 14, "Accessing Provincial Government Sources.")

- If you're searching for a monograph (material that is not a periodical, magazine, or bulletin), you can refer to the federal government's *Government of Canada Publications Quarterly Catalogue* and its *Weekly Checklist of Canadian Government Publications*. There is also the *Special List of Canadian Government Publications*, which highlights major publications, and the *Subject List*, which lists publications by subject. All of these guides are published by Canada's official government publisher, the Canadian Government Publishing Centre, a division of the Department of Supply and Services. These lists are often available at the government publications section of large public libraries.

  The Canadian Government Publishing Centre has a backlist of over 10,000 monographs, and most of these can be found in public depository libraries across Canada. To obtain a free list of these depositories, call the Publishing Centre at (819) 997-2560 and ask them to mail you a copy of the pamphlet, "Where and How to Obtain Canadian Government Publications."

  Associated bookstore agents sell these monographs, too. For a list of agents, contact the Publishing Centre and ask for a copy of their free brochure, "Associated Bookstore Agents for the Sale of Canadian Government Publications." The agents sell most major titles and have all the guides mentioned above, as well as a list of all previously published titles.

- Though you'll normally be successful in finding what you need either in the public library or directly from the department responsible for the publication, sometimes these routes will fail you. If so, you'll often be able to purchase a copy of the needed publication from Micromedia Limited, Toronto.

- In addition to publications that you have to purchase, there are also publications that are distributed *free of charge*. Each department has its own mailing list of people who receive these publications. For a list of federal departments, their addresses, and telephone numbers, call the Canadian Government Publishing Centre and request a copy of their pamphlet, "Government of Canada Information Services Free Publications," then call the appropriate department and ask to be placed on its mailing list.

  You can also use the contacts in this pamphlet to inquire about published materials other than monographs, such as limited distribution reports (described in Chapter 14, "Accessing Provincial Government Sources"). For example, *Innovation* can be of tremendous benefit to investors in the manufacturing industry. It is published quarterly by the Department of Regional Industrial Expansion "to inform Canadian industry of licensing and joint venture opportunities that may be investigated for the purpose of forming manufacturing affiliations." Anyone in the industry can obtain a free subscription by telephoning (613) 954-3458.

- If you are interested in finding out which companies have received federal government contracts, you can refer to the *Bulletin of Business Opportunities*, published by the federal Department of Supply and Services each week. The subscription rate is $153 per year, and you can sign up by calling (819) 956-3440. *CanadExport* is published bi-weekly by External Affairs's Trade Communications division and provides information on trade opportunities abroad, trade fairs and missions, and more. It's available free of charge by calling 1-800-267-8376. Or, say you want to know the amount of donations made to any of the three major political parties and who made them: refer to the *Registered Party Fiscal Period Returns* published by the Chief Electoral Officer (an *agency* of Parliament, not a department). A copy of this annual publication can be ordered at 1-800-267-8683.

KEEPING INFORMED ABOUT GOVERNMENT BUSINESS

The most popular way to keep informed about what is happening at the federal government level is by reading *Hansard*, the official transcript of all House of Commons proceedings. *Hansard*, plus a subject and personal name index, are kept at public libraries. You can purchase copies from government bookstore agents or directly from the Canadian Government Publishing Centre. (A similar service is available for the proceedings of the Senate.)

Another method of keeping informed about federal government business and regulations affecting private business is by referring to the weekly publication *Canada Gazette, Part One*. (Part Two of this publication lists all new government regulations, along with details of new federal acts, and appears every second week. Part Three, published irregularly, lists all new acts immediately after they have received royal assent.)

The *Ottawa Letter* is another good source of federal government information. It describes the activities of the executive, judicial, and legislative branches. Available at most libraries, it is published weekly in a loose-leaf format.

A similar service is *Canadian News Facts*, which provides a synopsis of important news items, including federal government news. It is also published on a bi-weekly basis in loose-leaf form by Marpep Publishing. It, too, can be found in most public libraries.

The Public Sector, published weekly by Southam Communications Ltd., provides an analysis of government policies, pending legislation, and new laws.

It is impossible in a book of this scope to provide more than a mere sampling of departmental sources at the federal government level. As is the case with provincial government sources, I have highlighted a few federal sources that have assisted me in my research. If you follow the guidelines presented at the beginning of this chapter, you should be able to tap additional sources as well.

DEPARTMENT OF CONSUMER AND CORPORATE AFFAIRS

You may require information on the legal status of a corporation because you're planning to lend it money, or perhaps you've just inherited some shares from a relative's estate. You may also need to verify whether a trademark has been registered or to examine or obtain copies of a balance sheet showing reported revenues, assets, and earnings of a public or private federally-registered corporation. You can acquire all this information over the telephone free of charge, as outlined below.

Corporations Branch   *All* federal corporations must file at least three forms in order to be incorporated under the Canada Business Corporations Act: Form 1: Articles of Incorporation; Form 3: Notice of Registered Office; and Form 6: Notice of Directors. These are reproduced in Figure 15.1. Basic information recorded on them can be obtained over the telephone by dialing the inquiries unit at (819) 997-1142. You can obtain uncertified copies at $1 per page and have these mailed to you by calling the photocopying area of the Corporations Branch at (819) 997-3462.

Federal corporations must comply with other filing requirements, too. All distributing (public) corporations and all non-distributing (private) corporations with assets of $5 million or revenues over $10 million must file an annual, audited financial statement. The Corporations Branch has between 5,000 and 6,000 of these financial statements on file, and although this number is small in comparison to the over 160,000 federal

Figure 15.1a   Sample Form 1: Articles of Incorporation

Consumer and Corporate Affairs Canada	Consommation et Corporations Canada	FORM 1 ARTICLES OF INCORPORATION (SECTION 6)	FORMULE 1 STATUTS CONSTITUTIFS (ARTICLE 6)
Canada Business Corporations Act	Loi sur les sociétés commerciales canadiennes		

1 – Name of Corporation   Dénomination de la société

2 – The place in Canada where the registered office is to be situated   Lieu au Canada où doit être situé le siège social

3 – The classes and any maximum number of shares that the corporation   Catégories et tout nombre maximal d'actions que la société est
is authorized to issue   autorisée à émettre

4 – Restrictions if any on share transfers   Restrictions sur le transfert des actions, s'il y a lieu

5 – Number (or minimum and maximum number) of directors   Nombre (ou nombre minimum et maximum) d'administrateurs

6 – Restrictions if any on business the corporation may carry on   Limites imposées quant aux activités commerciales que la société
peut exploiter, s'il y a lieu

7 – Other provisions if any   Autres dispositions s'il y a lieu

8 – Incorporators   Fondateurs

Names – Noms	Address (include postal code) Adresse (inclure le code postal)	Signature

FOR DEPARTMENTAL USE ONLY – À L'USAGE DU MINISTÈRE SEULEMENT
Corporation No. – N° de la société | Filed — Déposée

CCA-1385 (11-85)

Figure 15.1b   Sample Form 3: Notice of Registered Office

Consumer and Corporate Affairs Canada	Consommation et Corporations Canada	**FORM 3** — **NOTICE OF REGISTERED OFFICE OR NOTICE OF CHANGE OR REGISTERED OFFICE**
Canada Business Corporations Act	Loi sur les sociétés commerciales canadiennes	**FORMULE 3** — **AVIS DU LIEU DU SIÈGE SOCIAL OU AVIS DE CHANGEMENT DU LIEU DU SIÈGE SOCIAL**

1 – Name of Corporation – Dénomination de la société

2 – Corporation No. – No. de la société

3 – Address of the registered office   Adresse du siège social

4 – Effective date of change   Date effective du changement

5 – Previous address of the registered office   Adresse précédente du siège social

Date   Signature   Description of Office – Description du poste

CCA-1386 (4-86)

Figure 15.1c Sample Form 6: Notice of Directors

Consumer and Corporate Affairs Canada	Consommation et Corporations Canada	FORM 6	FORMULE 6
Canada Business Corporations Act	Loi sur les sociétés commerciales canadiennes	NOTICE OF DIRECTORS OR NOTICE OF CHANGE OF DIRECTORS	AVIS DES ADMINISTRATEURS OU AVIS DE CHANGEMENT DES ADMINISTRATEURS

1 — Name of Corporation — Dénomination de la société

2 — Corporation No. — N° de la société

3 — The following persons became directors of this corporation: Les personnes suivantes sont devenues administrateurs de la présente société:

Effective Date — Date d'entrée en vigueur

Name — Nom	Residential Address — Adresse résidentielle	Occupation	Citizenship Citoyenneté

4 — The following persons ceased to be the directors of this corporation: Les personnes suivantes ont cessé d'être administrateurs de la présente société:

Effective Date — Date d'entrée en vigueur

Name — Nom	Residential Address — Adresse résidentielle

5 — The directors of this corporation now are: Les administrateurs de la présente société sont maintenant

Name — Nom	Residential Address — Adresse résidentielle	Occupation	Citizenship Citoyenneté

Date	Signature	Description of Office — Description du poste

CCA-1388 (4/86)

corporations active in Canada, it does represent the most significant ones. A financial statement includes information on gross revenues, assets, net earnings, and other financial details. Upon payment of photocopying fees, it can be mailed to you. The assets, revenues and earnings can be disclosed over the telephone. You can also find out, by telephone, whether the annual returns, any changes of directors, or any changes of registered offices have been filed.

In a few rare instances, a corporation that is required to file a financial statement may obtain an exemption if it can prove to the Director of the Corporations Branch that the information may be detrimental to its business interests.

If one corporation amalgamates with another, it must file Form 9: Articles of Amalgamation. If it changes its corporate name, it must file Form 4: Articles of Amendment, along with the appropriate name-search report. There are over fifteen different forms that federally-incorporated companies may be required to file; however, Forms 1, 3, and 6 contain the information that all these businesses must file and these you can access quite easily.

The Corporations Branch maintains computer records on over 160,000 active federal corporations. In addition, it keeps track of 3,000,000 provincially-incorporated companies and trademark records using a computer system called NUANS. The Branch is now encouraging provincial authorities to provide machine-readable tapes of all provincially-registered sole proprietorships and partnerships for inclusion in the NUANS data base. At the time of this writing, it had incorporated these files for the provinces of Ontario, Manitoba, Saskatchewan, New Brunswick, Nova Scotia, and Prince Edward Island. Therefore, by telephoning the Branch and providing merely the name of a business, you can probably learn when the company began, whether or not it is federally or provincially incorporated or otherwise, and where to find the information you need.

Trade Marks Branch   If you want to find out who has registered a trademark or symbol for a product or service, telephone the Trade Marks Branch at (819) 997-1420. The staff will tell you the owner of the trademark, the company's name and address, and when any one of the more than 200,000 trademarks was registered with the Department of Consumer and Corporate Affairs. You can also ask for the name of the agent or representative of the owner of the trademark and any associated trademarks. There is no charge for a verbal reply; however, if you require photocopies of documents, you must visit the Trade Marks Branch in Hull, Quebec.

The Patent Branch   If you want to find out either if someone has filed a patent or how you can file a patent application, contact the Enquiries Section at (819) 997-1936.

The Copyright and Industrial Designs Branch   Call (819) 997-1725 for answers to questions concerning who has registered or how you can receive copyright protection and registration of industrial designs.

Bankruptcy Branch   There are several ways to find out whether a business or an individual has gone into bankruptcy. For a quick, verbal verification, telephone the local Bankruptcy Branch offices listed in the blue pages of your telephone directory.

The files are kept at any one of the fifteen local District Insolvency Offices, as well as at the Supreme Court of each province. The major documents include a list of the assets, liabilities, and dividends involved; Assignment of Bankruptcy forms; the Statement of Affairs; a Certificate of Appointment of Trustees; the notes of examination under oath (if an examination has been conducted); the minutes of the first meeting of creditors; and the trustees' Statement of Receipts and Disbursements.

Documents are maintained on file under the discharge of the trustee and are then sent to the archives. You can, therefore, visit the District Insolvency Office and inspect the documents if the bankruptcy is active. If it isn't, you can do a court record search.

Bureau of Competition Policy   The Marketing Practices branch of the Bureau of Competition Policy publishes a useful quarterly publication, *Misleading Advertising Bulletin*. The bulletin provides a list of all convictions under the misleading advertising and deceptive marketing practices provisions of the Competition Act and lists the name of the accused, the location of the offence, and the disposition. You can then follow up any case by accessing the full court record. The bulletin is available at some of the larger public libraries and at most law libraries.

Statistics Canada   Statistics Canada, on behalf of the federal government, works with every aspect of statistical information. The department publishes a broad range of materials, and no matter what your topic, there is usually an expert statistician who can either provide you with the information you need or give you advice on how to get it.

For example, a CBC producer once hired me to investigate the moving business in Canada. Among other things, he wanted to know how many people moved each year. This wasn't as easy a question to answer as it seemed. However, as you can see in Figure 15.2, the staff at Statistics Canada made a sincere effort to gather data for me and actually came up with more detailed information than I was originally seeking. This demonstrates the extent of the information you can gather by contacting the right civil servant.

Most of the staff in this department is based in Ottawa, although there are Statistics Canada offices located across the country. An extremely useful guide for finding the best experts is *A User Guide: Who to Contact at Statistics Canada.* You can order a free copy by writing to: Public Affairs Section, Statistics Canada, Third Floor, R. H. Coats Building, Tunneys Pasture, Ottawa, Ontario K1A 0T6. You can also call your nearest Statistics Canada office, at the following toll-free numbers:

- Alberta: 1-800-282-3907

- Southern Alberta (Calgary): 1-800-472-9708

- British Columbia (except Atlin, B.C.): 1-800-663-1551

- Manitoba: 1-800-542-3404

- Newfoundland and Labrador: 1-800-563-4255

- Northwest Territories: (call collect) (403) 495-3028

- Nova Scotia, New Brunswick, and Prince Edward Island: 1-800-565-7192

- Ontario: 1-800-268-1151

- Quebec: 1-800-361-2831

- Saskatchewan: 1-800-667-7164

- Yukon (and Atlin, B.C.): Zenith 08913

You can also call the above numbers and ask for the department's publications list. Some of the booklets, such as *Answers to Questions on Labour Statistics: A Union Guide,* can help you interpret statistics.

Figure 15.2a Statistics Canada Response to Information Request—
Letter

Statistics Statistique
Canada Canada

Ottawa, Canada

K1A OT6

February 6, 1984

Mr. Steve Overbury,
"Market Place",
Canadian Broadcasting Corporation,

Toronto, Ontario
M4P 2A4

Dear Mr. Overbury:

You will find attached a document summarizing the situation of the
household goods moving activity between 1973 and 1980. It has to
be understood that the For-hire Trucking Survey from which these
estimates have been produced covers only the non-local movement
(more than 25 kilometres) of companies that had earned $100,000 or
more of intercity transportation revenue during the preceding year.
Therefore, the figures presented in the attached table underestimate
the total measure of the activity. We do not think, however, that
this situation should significantly affect the interpretation of the
statistics. For a detailed description of the For-hire Trucking Survey, its coverage and methodology please consult the publication
"For-hire Trucking Survey" (Catalogue 53-224) Furthermore, please
note that the attached table refers only to the inter-provincial movement of household goods (i.e. intra-provincial movement has been
excluded).

If you need further assistance, or if you have any questions do not
hesitate to call Mr. Steven Mozes or Mr. Yvan Deslauriers at 1-613-
995-1976.

Yours truly,

Barbara J. Slater

Barbara J. Slater,
Director,
Transportation and Communications Division

Att.

Canada

Figure 15.2b   Statistics Canada Response to Information Request—
Data

Summary Statistics on the Inter-provincial, Inter-territorial and
Territorial/Provincial Transportation of
Used Household Goods within Canada

Year	Interprovincial, Inter-territorial and Territorial/Provincial Transportation of Used Household Goods by All Carriers		Interprovincial, Inter-Territorial and Territorial/Provincial Transportation of Used Household Goods by Van Line Affiliates		The Percentage of Interprovincial, Inter-territorial and Territorial/Provincial Transportation of Used Household Goods by Van Line Affiliates to All Carriers	
	Estimated ($) Revenues	CV(%)	Estimated ($) Revenues	CV(%)	Estimated (MS%) Market Share	CV(%)
1973	39,727,000	16.22	35,806,000	14.12	90.13	1.06
1974	42,928,000	4.77	37,642,000	0.48	87.69	2.15
1975	52,795,000	3.88	49,445,000	0.43	93.66	1.73
1976	69,590,000	1.09	65,144,000	4.35	93.61	1.63
1977	82,006,000	9.35	77,050,000	8.77	93.96	0.30
1978	87,978,000	1.81	84,036,000	0.62	95.52	0.59
1979	104,244,000	3.10	91,762,000	0.48	88.04	1.80
1980	111,562,000	4.01	102,907,000	0.59	92.24	2.30

MS: Market Share

CV: Coefficient of Variation

Note: This table is compiled from the annual For-hire Trucking Survey (Catalogue 53-224) and relates to the sector of the Motor Carrier Transportation Industry dealing with the inter-provincial, inter-territorial and territorial/provincial transportation of used household goods within Canada.

If you require information on the corporate structure of Canadian society, one of the best sources is a publication by Statistics Canada called *Inter-Corporate Ownership*. If there were a Pulitzer Prize for reference books, this publication would unquestionably be nominated. Under the brilliant guidance of Ronald Vanasse, the reference staff have made life immensely easier for researchers by producing this book. *Inter-Corporate Ownership*, available at most libraries, provides a detailed list of businesses in Canada, their subsidiaries, and the degree of any foreign ownership. It also includes information from the federal government's Corporation and Labour Unions Returns Act, the *Canada Gazette*, Investment Canada, newspaper and magazine articles, *Moody's, Standard and Poor's, Jane's*, and *Who Owns Whom*. At the time of this writing, the latest edition of *Inter-Corporate Ownership* was published in 1987.

The information contained in this publication is regularly updated on computer. If you are using the 1987 edition and require a single update, you can call Statistics Canada at (613) 951-3469 and ask for the information. The department does not update entries on a regular basis but does honour the occasional request; if you need updated information on a number of companies, there is a hefty charge. If you require up-to-date information regularly, it would be wise to subscribe to the "Inter-Corporate Ownership" data base, available in Canada from STM Systems Corp. of Toronto.

DEPARTMENT OF FINANCE

One source for finding out the indebtedness of a company or of individuals involved in a company is the Bank of Canada's registrations sytem. A provision under Section 178 of the federal Bank Act governs certain categories of loans made by any Canadian chartered bank to companies involved in various kinds of manufacturing, farming, fishing, and so forth. A chartered bank making a loan under Section 178 registers the information at one of the Bank's "agency point" offices.

You can conduct a search in person or mail in your request, along with $2 per name, at any one of these offices. The offices are located in Vancouver (for all of British Columbia, the Northwest Territories, and the Yukon), Calgary, Regina, Winnipeg, Toronto, Montreal, Halifax, and Saint John (for New Brunswick, Newfoundland, and Prince Edward Island).

You are then given the name of the business, the name of the owner, and the name and address of the chartered bank. Information on the amount of the loan or the branch of the bank is not available—to obtain it, you must contact the business directly. This information can alert you to the fact that some of the assets of a business are tied up in a loan.

LABOUR CANADA

As an employer or a representative of a union you no longer have to go any further than a one-stop information service for data relating to industrial relations or collective bargaining. The Bureau of Labour Information (BLI) is a centralized source whose wide range of services is readily available to you.

The Bureau, which was established in 1987, assembles its information from a number of sources including its own electronic database. BLI analyses more than 200 provisions in all contracts covering 500 or more workers. From this database, you can obtain spreadsheets of major agreements on a provision-by-provision basis for use in comparing contracts, or receive detailed listings or tabulations of agreements containing specific types of clauses. In addition, the Bureau of Labour Information can provide you with details on recent wage settlements in all major agreements in a particular industry or geographic area.

The Bureau also has an extensive industrial relations library and a collective agreement library. The latter stores approximately 8,000 federal and provincial agreements covering 100 or more employees. Other services available include work stoppage information, up to date federal and provincial labour-related legislation, arbitration decisions, corporate information, photocopies of contract language and other data.

In some instances you may be able to get information over the telephone or, if your need warrants, arrange an overnight courier service. The Bureau also produces a number of publications free of charge on a quarterly, monthly, or annual basis, which include the following:

- *Collective Bargaining Information Sources* Compiled annually, this publication is a concise and descriptive listing of over 400 publications and services of use to anyone involved in industrial relations or collective bargaining.

- *Access* This annual is a users' guide to federal programs and services of particular interest to the working people of Canada and their organizations.

- *Major Wage Settlements* This publication is a quarterly review of wage trends in major collective bargaining settlements.

- *Collective Bargaining Review* A summary of wage and non-wage provisions in major collective agreements, wage trends from collective bargaining, strikes and lockouts, occupational wage rates, working conditions, and other relevant items are all provided in this monthly.

The Bureau of Labour Information has a number of industrial relations consultants to serve you, each responsible for a different region in Canada. They can be reached toll free at 1-800-567-6866 or in the National Capital Region at (819) 997-3117.

All queries to the Bureau of Labour Information are kept strictly confidential.

NATIONAL ARCHIVES OF CANADA

If you're researching *any* aspect of Canadian life, don't overlook the vast amounts of publicly accessible resources at the National Archives of Canada. Located at 395 Wellington Street, Ottawa, the archives stores an endless array of Canadian and foreign material, including, as a promotional brochure states, "letters, accounts, telegrams, registers, reports, maps, globes, atlases, architectural plans, photographs, watercolours, engravings, sketches and drawings, oil paintings, computer tapes, sound recordings, films, and videocassettes."

Of special interest to those tracing their family history is the Manuscript Division of the archives which issues a free publication, *Tracing Your Ancestors in Canada*, which you can order by telephoning (613) 996-7458.

FREEDOM OF INFORMATION LAWS

Are you a civil servant who has been denied a promotion because of a negative report on file with your employer? Are you interested in what the government is doing behind the scenes? These kinds of questions and thousands more may be answered through our freedom of information laws. On July 1, 1983 two significant pieces of legislation—the Access to Information Act and a related statute, the Privacy Act—came into force. As is the case with many other of its laws, Canada, in enacting these laws, followed in the footsteps of other nations. In this instance the United States, which passed a Freedom of Information Act in 1966, provided the lead.

Our laws, however, have not been nearly as effective as those of other nations in opening government information vaults. In the United States information that is embarrassing or damaging to the government is released routinely. For example, when a U.S. cruiser gunned down an Iranian Airbus killing 290 people in the summer of 1988, U.S. Navy officials filmed the tragedy. That film was released within two months of the incident to television journalists who requested it under the Freedom of Information Act. This kind of openness is rare in Canada.

In 1987 under the scandal-ridden Tory government of Brian Mulroney, an all-party committee made 108 recommendations for more openness to both pieces of legislation. The recommendations were virtually ignored. Even Canada's Auditor General, Kenneth Dye, was denied access to government documents needed to complete his job as auditor. And the *Toronto Star* sadly learned, after having painstakingly pinpointed crucial documents relating to the abasement of Japanese Canadians during the Second World War, that the federal government said it could not release the information because the files had been destroyed.

My own personal experience using freedom of information laws in Canada has been mixed. For instance, I once requested a copy of a confidential clinical study on a hair restorer lotion known as "MJS." This lotion was registered with the Department of Health and Welfare as a drug. I knew that for it to be registered as such with this department, a clinical study proving its effectiveness had to be submitted, and I wanted to determine how thorough the study was. The access co-ordinator told me the study was commercial information of a confidential nature, and he would therefore have to contact the manufacturer of the lotion for permission to release it. I eventually obtained a copy of the study, but it took a few months, even though I had sent my application by courier and had conducted several telephone conversations with the access officer.

The episode taught me a lesson: if at all possible avoid getting information through our freedom of information laws. Most information is kept in more than one place. I should have contacted the manufacturer from the start to get the confidential study. After all, he did agree to release it to me through the government.

Although the original intent of Canada's freedom of information laws was to make it easier to access government information, in practice this does not always happen. In fact, sometimes the reverse happens. For example, I once requested from the Department of Supplies and Services a list of all companies that had won major contracts to build and/or repair federal government vessels. I needed the information in a hurry but was told I would have to apply for it under the Access to Information Act. Instead, I made several calls to other sources that kept this information and learned that it was contained in the *Public Accounts of Canada*, a copy of which I secured in the public library!

If you are having difficulty finding other avenues for obtaining information, and if you have plenty of patience, our freedom of information laws may unlock your information needs. What follows is a more exact account of how the laws work.

Privacy Act   Before the Privacy Act was passed, Canadians had some access to the files the federal government kept on them and some protection over who had access to the information, under Part Four of the Canadian Human Rights Act (which has been in effect since March 1, 1978). The Privacy Act both expands the access to and increases the protection of personal information on individuals beyond the bounds that previously existed.

You can obtain copies of, or examine, any personal information on yourself collected for a federal government program or operation. (There are, of course, certain exemptions, such as any information pertaining to national security or law enforcement agencies. However, government officials in many instances now have to provide reasons for the denial of information.) If there are factual errors in the information, you may have them corrected by contacting the department that collected them. As well, if there is a dispute over the interpretation of reported events, you may have your version put in the file.

To pursue this information begin by visiting any large public library, or in smaller communities visit the local post office, and obtain the brochure describing the service and how to use it, "Access To Information Act and Privacy Act." You can also pick up a simple application form, which is reproduced in Figure 15.3. Another useful tool is the *Personal Information Index*, which provides a detailed breakdown of most federal government departments and agencies, along with lists of the types of information each collects. The *Index* can be found in most public libraries or may be purchased from any authorized federal government bookstore for a nominal fee. Using it, you must single out the department and sub-department in order to identify the information you require and where it is kept.

No processing fee is charged for providing this information. The federal government is legally bound to reply to your request within thirty days of receiving your application, although it can extend this limit to an additional thirty days or more for a number of reasons.

There is an appeal mechanism. If information is outright or partially denied, or personal information is being disposed of in a manner with which you find fault, or if you have any other complaint, you may by all means send a letter to the Office of the Privacy Commissioner. Your letter will be acted upon.

Access to Information Act   This statute, for the first time in Canadian legal history, gives Canadian citizens and permanent residents the legal right to examine, or obtain copies of, records of federal government institutions. This information includes a broad range of data—from press releases issued by government agencies to detailed expenditures of cabinet ministers. Of course, anything relating to national security or trade secrets is exempt.

For anyone who plans to use this law, it is advisable to visit any large library (or post offices in small communities) and read the pamphlet, "Access to Information Act and Privacy Act." Included with the pamphlet is a simple application form (reproduced in Figure 15.4) and the *Access Registry*, which provides an organizational outline of the federal government and details of the information banks of each department or agency. The *Access Registry* is kept in most public libraries and can be purchased through any bookstore authorized by the federal government.

Figure 15.3   Sample Personal Information Request Form

I✶ Government   Gouvernement
of Canada   du Canada

Privacy Act

Personal Information Request Form

For official use only

Individuals are required to use this form to request access to personal information about themselves under the Privacy Act.

STEP 1: *Decide whether or not you wish to submit a request under the Privacy Act.* You may decide to request the information informally, without using the procedures required by the Act, through the local office of the appropriate government institution or through the Privacy Co-ordinator listed in the Index of Personal Information. Copies of the Index are available in public libraries, post offices in rural areas and government information offices.

STEP 2: *Consult the Index of Personal Information.* If you have decided to exercise your rights of access under the Privacy Act, review the descriptions of personal information for institutions which are most likely to have the information you are seeking. Decide on the personal information bank or class of personal information likely to contain the information.

STEP 3: *Complete this personal information request form.* Indicate the personal information bank or class of personal information to which you are requesting access, and include any additional information indicated in the bank description to locate the information you are seeking, or to verify

your own identity. Indicate whether you wish to receive copies of the information, examine the original in a government office, or if you are requesting other arrangements for access. There is no application fee for making a request under the Privacy Act.

STEP 4: *Send the request to the person identified in the Index* as the appropriate officer responsible for the particular personal information bank or class.

STEP 5: *Review the information you received in response to your request.* Decide if you wish to make further requests under the Privacy Act. You may wish to exercise your rights to request corrections or to require that notations be attached to the information when corrections are not made. You may also decide to complain to the Privacy Commissioner when you believe that you have been denied any of your rights under the Act.

Federal Government Institution

Registration Number and Personal Information Bank or Class of Personal Information

I wish to examine the information ☐ As it is   ☐ All in English   ☐ All in French

Provide other details specified in the Index to aid in locating particular information or to verify identity of applicant. (Present or former members of the Canadian Armed Forces requesting military records must provide additional information as specified in the D.N.D. section of the Index.)

Method of access preferred
☐ Receive copies of the original   ☐ Examine original in government office   ☐ Other method (please specify)

Identification of applicant
Name (or previous name)

Social Insurance No. (or other identifying no. if applicable)

Street address, apartment

City or town

Province, territory, or other

Postal Code

Telephone number(s)

If this request follows a previous enquiry, quote reference number ➤

I have a right of access to personal information about myself under the Privacy Act by virtue of my status as a Canadian citizen, a permanent resident within the meaning of the Immigration Act, 1976, or by Order of the Governor in Council pursuant to subsection 12(3) of the Privacy Act.

Signature

Date

Canadä

Français au verso

TBC 350-58 (Rev. 85/8)

Figure 15.4 Sample Access to Information Request Form

Government **Gouvernement**
of Canada **du Canada**

Access to Information Act

Access to Information Request Form

For official use only

Use of this form will help speed your access to *records* **under the Access to Information Act. Requests for federal government** *information* **can ordinarily be made by means of a telephone call, a visit, or a written request to the appropriate government information office. There is a fee of $5.00 for making a formal request under the Access to Information Act.**

STEP 1: *Decide exactly what information you want* — You can facilitate the search for records and reduce fees by defining as narrowly as you can the particular records you are looking for.

STEP 2: *Consult the Access Register* — The register contains descriptions of government records, their probable location and other information which will likely assist you in identifying the particular records you wish to see. A copy of the Access Register is available at major libraries, post offices, and government information offices.

STEP 3: *Ask for assistance if necessary* — If you are unable to identify the records you are looking for in the Access Register, contact the Access Co-ordinator of the appropriate department, either in person, by telephone or by letter at the address shown in the Register. The Co-ordinator will assist you in identifying the records.

STEP 4: *Complete this Request Form,* providing as many specific details as you can about the desired records, such as:
— subject, title and date;
— specific events, activities, individuals, corporations, products, reports, meetings, decisions, agreements, etc., of interest in the records;
— the number and title of the appropriate class of records, as listed in the Access Register.

STEP 5: *Send in the completed Request Form or written request with an application fee of* $5.00, payable by money order or cheque to the Receiver General of Canada, to the appropriate officer identified in the Access Register. Unless you have already indicated what you are willing to pay for, you will be asked to authorize any fees that may be charged before the work is completed.

Federal Government Department, Agency or Crown Corporation

Identification number and title of class(es) of record(s) (see step 2)

Description of records and topics of interest (see step 4)

I wish to:
☐ Receive copies of the original   ☐ Examine original in government office   ☐ Other method (please specify)

Identification of applicant
Name

Street address, apartment   City or town

Province, territory or other   Postal Code   Telephone number(s)

I have a right of access to government records under the Access to Information Act by virtue of my status as a Canadian citizen, a permanent resident within the meaning of the Immigration Act, 1976, or by Order of the Governor in Council pursuant to subsection 4(2) of the Access to Information Act.

Signature   Date

Canada

Français au verso   TBC 350-57 (Rev. 85/8)

As with the Privacy Act, you should spend some time reading the *Access Registry* to identify the information bank that stores the information you require. The *Access Registry* also lists addresses of access co-ordinators who will be handling your request. To speed up your application, which can take over eighty days to process, *telephone* the access coordinator— before you send in your application—to make sure you have listed the proper descriptive information. The access co-ordinator can help you complete the form and tell you how long it will take to complete the process, as well as advising you of your chances of obtaining the information. This initial discussion can also give you an idea of the approximate volume of material you are requesting. Because there is a five-dollar fee to read your application, an additional ten-dollar-per-hour charge for requests that involve over five hours of research, along with further charges for photocopying the material, an estimate at this stage is very helpful.

What are the odds of your success in obtaining information using the Access to Information Act? One survey found that of 12,000 requests, forty-two percent of applicants received all of the information requested. If you are denied information, or if the government unduly delays processing your request or charges you an excessive fee, send a letter to the Information Commissioner. A survey showed that one of every nine users of the act contacted this office for help. The Commissioner can appeal your case to the Federal Court of Appeal, which it has done in the past and won, thereby overruling the federal government.

For further insight into the ins and outs of our freedom of information laws I recommend an easy to read and inexpensive paperback, *Using the Access to Information Act*, published by International Self-Counsel Press. Written by two concerned lawyers, Heather Mitchell and Murray Rankin, it covers both pieces of legislation.

Unravelling Court Records

Court record searches can be either a researcher's dream or nightmare. A crucial advantage to such searches is that a court record may contain confidential information on individuals or businesses that is not available anywhere else. The problem is that access to these records is a great uncertainty and varies considerably from court to court. Some courts won't even allow you to sit in on civil or criminal proceedings, or examine the most basic documents, unless you're an involved party. Other courts allow you to attend legal proceedings and examine documents.

It's a good idea right from the start to consult either the local court Registrar or the Clerk of the court to establish the court's policy. For a list of court offices across Canada, refer to the *Canadian Law List*. This is an annual publication available at many libraries.

If you are denied access to court proceedings or records, you may have to rely on one of the lawyers involved to obtain the information for you or, as a last resort, you may have to go to court to force the government to give access.

It is unlikely, however, that you would have to use court records on more than the odd occasion. In fact, I can think of only two instances where court records gave me information that might not otherwise have been available.

While working as a journalist, I once wanted to know if the giant shoe manufacturer, Bata Industries Limited, was involved in the production of tank equipment for the United States Army. Interviews with various Bata officials, including Thomas Bata himself, didn't answer my question. However, an obscure court record, an affidavit filed by a senior Bata executive to obtain an injunction against picketing strikers, revealed that the company was indeed heavily involved in the defence industry.

On another occasion I required financial information on a privately owned, international soap company. I also needed background information on one of the firm's executives. By accessing this person's divorce records, I was able to glean both types of usually confidential information.

Despite the seemingly complex court network in Canada, I was able to locate the court records in both cases, because I understood the basic structure and jurisdictions of the courts and knew the types of documents that existed. Without this overview, my job would have been like searching for a needle in a haystack.

A word of caution: avoid "fishing expeditions" with the staff at a court. If you show up at a county court and ask for assistance before you've narrowed down your request, don't expect much help. Here is an example of a vague request: "My father was involved in some sort of legal action in western Canada in the last few decades. Where can I find his files?"

You would stand a far better chance of accessing court records with a request like this: "My father, Sam J. Orez, was divorced in Toronto in 1979. Where can I find the court records for this divorce?"

This latter question is much more refined and therefore far easier to answer. The local litigation clerk or registrar should gladly assist you with such a question. The question pertains to a *civil* proceeding involving a divorce, which means that the records would be kept at the Supreme Court office for the judicial district of York. With the date of the divorce and the name of one of the parties involved, it is possible to pull the file for this case.

In other words, the secret to unravelling court records is to focus on the proper nature of the case, the jurisdiction of the court, and, eventually, the particular document you need.

STRUCTURE AND JURISDICTION

The first chapter of Clare Beckton's book, *The Law and the Media*, gave me a good overview of the structure of Canadian courts. There are two levels of courts in Canada—federal and provincial. The Supreme Court of Canada is the country's final court of appeal for criminal and civil cases. In addition, there is the Federal Court, with a trial division (where cases are heard) and an appeal division. The Federal Court is responsible for such areas of law as immigration, citizenship, and taxation. Under the Constitution Act, 1867, provinces are vested with the power to establish their own courts. The names of these courts vary in different provinces, but their structure is essentially the same.

In order to begin searching for a court record, you must first understand if the case was a *civil* or *criminal* proceeding.

Civil Courts   Civil cases involve breaches of the relationship between persons; the amount of money involved in a claim helps to determine which court hears the case. However, most civil cases are settled out of court, after an *examination for discovery* or *discoveries*—a pretrial meeting where both parties obtain details from each other to determine if they will proceed to trial.

The civil court structure is as follows:

- *Small Claims Courts* handle disputes involving $3,000 or less.

- *County Courts* or *District Courts* handle disputes up to $25,000.

- The provincial *Queen's Bench* or *Supreme Court* handles disputes involving large settlements. In Ontario, for example, such settlements involve $25,000 or more. However, certain cases, such as libel, slander, and bankruptcy are automatically heard at this level.

- Any appeals from these courts can be heard by the various provincial courts of appeal.

- There are a variety of "specialty courts" from province to province. These exist according to the needs of each province. They can include *Family Courts*, which hear cases involving juveniles and families, and *Surrogate* or *Probate Courts*, which handle the administration of wills and estates.

Criminal Courts   Criminal cases involve crimes against society or individuals, and these crimes are described in various federal and provincial statutes. A key piece of legislation is the *Criminal Code of Canada*, under which there are *summary convictions* (which involve less serious crimes, such as theft under $200) and *indictable offences* (which involve the most serious offences, such as rape and murder).

The nature of the crime determines which level of court hears a criminal proceeding. Criminal laws are administered through the provinces at one of these levels of court:

- The *Provincial Court* or *Magistrates Court* hears most criminal cases—all summary convictions as well as some indictable offences.

  In the case of certain crimes, such as armed robbery, the accused has the right to choose to be tried at the Provincial Court level or at either of the higher courts—the County Court or Supreme Court. If the accused chooses a higher court, he or she may undergo a *preliminary hearing* at the Provincial Court level to determine if there is enough evidence to proceed to trial. The accused can also waive a preliminary hearing by admitting in court that there is sufficient evidence to make a committal.

  If an individual is accused of a more serious crime, such as murder, he or she is automatically tried by a higher court.

- *County Courts* or *District Courts* hear criminal matters such as drug trafficking, arson, burglary, and criminal negligence. Appeals from summary conviction may also be heard here. This level of criminal court is sometimes referred to as a *Superior Court*.

- The provincial *Queen's Bench* or *Supreme Court* (trial division) is the highest level of court for criminal trials in each province. It hears the most serious crimes and, through its appeal division, also hears appeals from the lower courts. It is known in some provinces as a *Superior Court*.

IDENTIFYING DOCUMENTS

With some understanding of the structure and jurisdiction of Canadian courts, you can determine the most logical place for records to be kept. You should also be aware of what types of documents exist, in order to restrict your search to those that can answer your questions. In this section a sampling of the key civil and criminal documents is provided.

Keep in mind that if a legal proceeding has been *completed*, most ofthe documents concerning it are contained in one file or in a batch of files kept in one court house. Also, older records are kept in various storage facilities; ask the staff in charge of records where they are located and how to access them.

If you intend to use any documents for publication purposes, be careful—another party may have made an application for an order restraining publication. Journalists beware: *make sure that no such order exists before publishing any court records.* If you ignore such an order, you may be subject to contempt of court or libel proceedings. In addition, check to see that there aren't any *further* statutory provisions in your jurisdiction or in the Criminal Code preventing you from publishing particular kinds of information. These statutory provisions vary from province to province.

The documents discussed below are common to most provinces, although some variations may be found in Quebec. Ask the staff in charge of records at the court concerned to clarify the name and contents of the documents you seek.

Civil Documents   To access records from a civil case, begin with the name of one of the parties involved. (In legal jargon this is known as the *style of cause.*) Using a name, you can search through the annual Matters Index Books (usually kept near the main counter of the court office that stores legal records) for a *writ number* or a *statement of claim number.* (In some provinces, such as Ontario, writs are no longer issued. Instead, a statement of claim is used.) Civil court records in Canada are filed under one of these two reference numbering systems.

Cases are filed in the Matters Index Books by the surname of the person suing, followed by the surname of the person being sued. (Different courts label the parties differently—as the plaintiff versus the defendant, applicant versus respondent, or petitioner versus respondent.) It is therefore easier to use these alphabetically organized annual indexes if you have the plaintiff's name. But even with the defendant's name you can still find the reference number, although your search will take longer.

Once you have the reference number, simply approach the front counter of the court house and ask to see the appropriate files, which you can view on the premises. There isn't normally a fee to examine most court records, although there are photocopying charges.

The following are the main types of documents you can expect to find in a court file:

- A *statement of claim* is filed in court to initiate legal action, and it outlines precisely what the aggrieved person is claiming. Various counterclaims may be registered as well. And don't accept a statement of claim at face value: always follow through on the case by checking to see what the final judgement, ruling, or court order was.

- A *statement of defence* is a written reply to the statement of claim.

- A *writ of summons* is issued to the person being sued. It states the damages incurred, what compensation is being sought, and gives the name and address of the person being sued.

- The *discovery of documents* is a meeting where both parties provide each other with pertinent documents to the case. These can include a broad range of materials, such as invoices, letters, and insurance agreements. Once these are submitted to the examination for discovery, they may or may not be declared as *exhibits*.

- An *examination for discovery* is a meeting where both parties cross-examine each other and present evidence and counterevidence to determine if the case should proceed to pretrial and trial. If one of the lawyers involved in the case requests and pays for a copy of the minutes of this meeting from the court, a copy will also be provided in the public file.

- A *pretrial* is held after the examination for discovery to try to settle the matter out of court. If a settlement is made, and one of the parties has requested the *minutes of settlement*, these minutes are filed in court as well. They outline what the precise settlement was. If there was an order made by a judge, that order is also recorded.

- *Motions* of various kinds may be heard by legal tribunals before a trial takes place. A motion may, for example, include adding parties and amending the pleadings, and it is heard before a *master* at *master's court*. A master doesn't have the full authority of a judge, and these decisions may be overturned. The master files a *master's report* outlining the judgement on a motion.

  Other kinds of motions, such as various forms of injunctions, are heard before a judge at *motions court* (sometimes called a *weekly court*). Records of any *interim orders* made are kept on file. You may also find various affidavits (sworn statements), judgements, and rulings on motions in the file.

  If you want to know only the outcome of a motion, look for the *motion record*. On the back of this document is a handwritten endorsement or denial of the motion by either a master or a judge.

- *Minutes of the trial* are generally prepared, along with affidavits, and these are generally available.

- *Judgements*, *orders*, and *endorsements* are recorded and filed. You may find that some courthouses keep judgements separately on microfilm, not in the general file.

- A *writ of execution* (*writ of seizure and sale* in Ontario) is an extremely useful post-court document. You can find this document in the general file or through the sheriff at the County or District Court office. A writ of execution flows from a court judgement and empowers the sheriff to seize and sell assets of a debtor, including real and personal property, because the individual has defaulted on payments.

  With a name and an approximate date, you can search for this document at the sheriff's office. You can also obtain an abstract of the court judgement there. However, to access the full file, look for the court records in the court where the case was heard.

  A writ of execution does not state if the person has paid what the court has ordered, but it does indicate to a prospective buyer that there is a registered judgement against some of his or her real or personal property.

- *Last wills and testaments* are filed in Surrogate Court, a division of the County Court. With a name and an approximate date, you can obtain a copy of a will.

Criminal Records   Criminal records are always more difficult to obtain than records of civil cases, and in most instances you have to give the court clerical staff a valid reason for examining them. (There is, however, no hard-and-fast rule about what constitutes a valid reason.) In nearly every instance you require some significant identifying features of the case, such as the full name of the accused, the date of the court proceeding, the level of court, and its geographic location.

If you do not have such details, you may be able to find them in newspaper accounts or from one of the lawyers involved in the case. If a judgement was rendered, you can search through the *Weekly Criminal Bulletin*, published by the Canada Law Book Incorporated. This publication gives an abstract of many criminal cases, including identifying pieces of information. (There is also an equivalent publication for civil cases, the *All-Canada Weekly Summaries*. Most libraries keep both of these.)

If you have enough information to identify a case to the staff at the court involved and need only to check the disposition of the legal proceeding, telephone the court directly. It is easier to obtain this information by telephone than it is to actually see the documents described below:

- The *information* is the document in which the accused is charged. It includes the name of the accused, age, address, and sometimes occupation.

- The *indictment* is another charging document, containing the same information. Once a person is committed to trial following a preliminary hearing, an indictment is prepared and serves as the basis for further proceedings.

- A *search warrant* is the document giving law enforcement officials the legal right to search a specific premise and to seize specific things.

- The *information to obtain a search warrant* is much more revealing than the search warrant itself. It includes an affidavit by the police officer involved, explaining why the police department believes a crime is being committed and how the warrant will help solve the crime. A Supreme Court of Canada ruling has made this document public information if the police have in fact seized what they set out to seize.

  Unfortunately, there is no central depository for this information, but generally it is kept at the Provincial Court. Ask the court staff for assistance in locating this document.

- The *transcript of a preliminary hearing* can also be revealing. A preliminary hearing takes place before a judge of a Provincial Court to determine whether there is sufficient evidence to proceed to trial. The transcript can be ordered from the court reporter, and this can be an expensive undertaking. You may, however, be able to borrow a copy of the transcript from one of the lawyers involved in the case.

- A *transcript of the trial* is available whenever a case goes to trial and may include testimonies of any witnesses. Again, you may have to pay a court reporter to transcribe a copy for you.

- *Exhibits* are usually filed in court as evidence of a person's innocence or guilt. Exhibits include any kind of physical evidence, from fingerprints on a glass to furniture. Exhibits are generally returned to their owners shortly after a court action has been completed, but some may be kept in a court file or in storage. Ask the court staff if they have any exhibits in storage.

- *Judgements, rulings,* and *orders* are crucial documents that state the final disposition of a case unless the decision is appealed. Judgements may be included in a general court file along with other court documents, but sometimes they are kept separately on microfilm. Ask the court staff about this.

- *Appeals on judgements* are sometimes made, and the results of the appeal are recorded in a document.

- *Bail hearings* are held to determine if the accused can be released from jail and under what conditions. The minutes of the proceedings may be filed if someone orders a transcript.

- *Bail Order Release Papers* are issued when the accused is released from custody. The release papers state any conditions or restrictions that may be attached to the release, such as a surety or recognizance. For example, the accused may not be allowed to go near a particular person or place. If an accused person is released into the custody of another person, that person's name and address are stated in the document.

- *Presentence reports* are prepared by probation services to help determine the appropriate sentence for the accused. These documents are extremely difficult to obtain unless you are one of the solicitors involved in the case.

- *Motions* of various kinds can be introduced at different times during the litigation process. For example, if there is a lot of adverse publicity before a trial, the lawyers of the accused might file a motion for a change of venue in an attempt to have the trial moved to another location.

  To establish the outcome of a motion, look on the back of the *motion record*, where you will find a judge's handwritten endorsement or denial of the motion.

For additional information on criminal court matters, I recommend *A Reporter's Guide to Canada's Criminal Justice System* by Harold J. Levy, published by the Canadian Bar Foundation (Suite 1700, 130 Albert Street, Ottawa K1P 5G4).

Bibliography

The following is a list of reference materials that I have acquired and used in an eclectic manner over the years; I have included a personal assessment of some of them. They have been used to meet my own information needs and do not constitute a definitive list of reference sources. I list them mainly to show the *range* of materials available and in the hope that they will stimulate the researcher to discover other useful reference works.

BUSINESS

Building The Strategic Plan: Find, Analyze and Present the Right Information. By Stephanie K. Marrus, published by John Wiley & Sons in 1984.

Business Competitor Intelligence: Methods for Collecting, Organizing, and Using Information. By William L. Sammon, Mark A. Kurland, and Robert Spitalnic, published by John Wiley & Sons in 1984. Contains contributions from twelve specialists who provide analyses of competitive intelligence.

Canadian Business Corporations Act and Regulations. Published annually by Richard de Boo, Don Mills, Ontario. Explains how the act works and provides all the forms that businesses must complete.

Canadian Key Business Directory. Published annually by Dun and Bradstreet. Provides basic data about large Canadian businesses.

Canadian Mines Handbook and *Canadian Oil and Gas Handbook.* Published each year by the Toronto-based Northern Miner Press. Includes company information on businesses involved in these industries.

Canadian Oil Register. Published annually by Southam Communications. Lists companies and key personnel in the oil industry.

Canadian Trade Index. Published annually by the Toronto-based Canadian Manufacturers' Association. Provides a useful survey of Canada's manufacturers whose products have more than local distribution.

The *Card Service.* One of many useful services offered by the Financial Post Information Service; published by The Financial Post Company Limited of Toronto. Includes in-depth profiles of hundreds of publicly-owned Canadian companies on handy index cards. Updated regularly.

Competitive Strategy: Techniques for Analyzing Industries and Competitors. By Michael E. Porter; published by The Free Press in 1980. Contains an excellent section on conducting an industry analysis. One of numerous books by Porter who is considered a guru in the world of competitive intelligence analysis.

Competitor Intelligence: How To Get It—How To Use It. By Leonard M. Fuld; published in 1985 by John Wiley & Sons. An excellent guide on how to research companies, although sources are American.

Corporate Loyalty: A Trust Betrayed. By Brian A. Grosman; published by Viking in 1988. Provides some serious thought on ethical and legal questions of obtaining competitor intelligence from former employees.

Directory of Canadian Chartered Accountants. Published by the Toronto-based Institute of Chartered Accountants.

Directory of Directors. Published each year by The Financial Post Company Limited. Lists key Canadian business people and their backgrounds. Very useful for anyone wanting to research interlocking directorships.

F & S Index International Annual. Published each year by Predicasts, Cleveland, Ohio; indexes over 750 business publications, newspapers, and reports on companies, products, and industries around the world.

Fraser's Canadian Trade Directory. Published annually by Maclean Hunter in four volumes. An exhaustive list of Canadian manufacturers, wholesalers, agents, and distributors with addresses, trade names, and foreign representatives.

How to Check Out Your Competition. By John M. Kelly; published by John Wiley & Sons in 1987. This is a how-to book, geared to the U.S. market.

How to Find Information About Companies. By Washington Researchers. Another do-it-yourself guide to researching companies in the U.S.

How to Incorporate a Small Business. By Mel Montgomery; published by Practical Small Business Publications, Vancouver. Everything you need to know about small businesses in B.C.

How to Invest in Canadian Securities. Published by the Toronto-based Canadian Securities Institute, the educational organization of the Canadian securities industry. Recommended reading for understanding how public companies raise money.

Inter-Corporate Ownership. Published by Statistics Canada every couple of years. Reveals the degree of foreign ownership and the corporate structure of companies operating in Canada. An invaluable source.

Investment Terms and Definitions. Published on an ongoing basis by the Canadian Securities Institute.

Moody's Investors Service, a company of the Dun and Bradstreet Corporation, Jersey City, N.J.; publishes a variety of manuals each year that carry basic data on businesses and corporations world-wide.

Scott's Industrial Directories contain a wealth of information on manufacturers and their agents, wholesalers, distributors, transportation companies, and special services related to the industry. There are four different directories in the series. Published by Southam Communications about every two years.

Survey of Industrials, Survey of Mines and Energy Resources, and *Survey of Predecessor and Defunct Companies.* Three excellent directories published annually by The Financial Post Company Limited. These contain a great deal of information on publicly-owned Canadian corporations, including those that are no longer active.

The Financial Analysts Federation Membership Directory. Published by the Financial Analysts Federation, New York, N.Y. Includes Canadian members in some major cities. Good source for locating experts in financial concerns.

Who Owns Whom in North America. Published annually by Dun and Bradstreet; shows the structure of companies, including a list of subsidiaries and associated companies. Other similar books published by Dun and Bradstreet include basic information on businesses in the United Kingdom and the Republic of Ireland.

COMPUTERS

Business Online: The Canadian Professional's Guide To Electronic Information Sources. Published in 1989 by John Wiley & Sons. Produced by Ulla de Stricker and Jane Dysart; recommended reading if you plan to do on-line searching.

Canadian Machine Readable Databases: A Directory and Guide. Compiled by Helen Rogers for the National Library of Canada, lists full names of Canadian databases, subject and other important information.

Database Canada. A bi-monthly Canadian newsletter produced in Toronto. Monitors Canadian and foreign vendors to evaluate their Canadian content. Great for screening sources.

Databook Directory of OnLine Services. Published by McGraw-Hill Information Systems in a mammoth two-volume, loose-leaf format. Profiles Canadian and foreign databases and their vendors. Regularly updated.

The Espial Canadian Database Directory. Published by Espial Productions of Toronto. Useful data on key Canadian data bases.

GOVERNMENT

A User Guide: Who to Contact at Statistics Canada. An extremely useful directory for anyone who wants to tap into the experts at Statistics Canada. Lists all key department heads. Available free through the Public Affairs Section of Statistics Canada.

Annual Report of the Provincial Auditor of Ontario. Printed annually by the Queen's Printer, Toronto. Each province has an equivalent publication which summarizes the findings of the provincial auditor's audit of the public accounts. Information on the spending practices of the provincial government, any improper administrative and accounting procedures, and recommendations for further government efficiency. Generally available from provincial government bookstores.

Canadian News Facts. Published bi-weekly by Marpep Publishing, Toronto. Provides a synopsis of important news items, including information on the federal government.

Corpus Administrative Index. Published by Southam Communications, Don Mills, Ontario. Lists key personnel of provincial and federal governments and their telephone numbers. This is one of several Corpus publications which deal with who's who in government.

Corpus Almanac & Canadian Sourcebook. Published annually by Southam Communications; contains a wealth of information on Canada, including government addresses and telephone numbers across the country. An excellent reference tool in two volumes.

Freedom of Information and Protection of Privacy Act. Published by Insight Educational Services of Toronto. Loose-leaf format; provides addresses which were presented by a variety of speakers on November 25, 1985.

Government of Canada Telephone Directory National Capital Region. Published by Communications Canada's Government Telecommunications Agency; available from the Canadian Government Publishing Centre, Ottawa, or from associated bookstore agents. (Five other volumes for the Ontario, Pacific, Atlantic, Prairie, and Quebec regions are also published. These six telephone books contain every federal government telephone number across the country).

Index to Federal Programs and Services. Published annually by the Canadian Government Publishing Centre. Includes information on federal departments, agencies, and Crown corporations, and addresses and telephone numbers of federal government offices across Canada. Highly recommended.

Microlog. Published monthly by Micromedia Limited, Toronto, with a cumulative index at the end of each year. Is an index of reports from all levels of government and institutional sources.

Ottawa Letter. Published weekly by CCH Canadian Limited, Toronto. A wide assortment of useful information on behind-the-scenes happenings in the federal government.

Personal Information Index. Published by the Minister of Supply and Services, Ottawa. Describes the personal information under the control of the federal government. Most public libraries keep a copy.

Provincial Legislative Record. Published by CCH Canadian Ltd. Lists provincial government bills that are introduced in Parliament.

Public Accounts of Canada. Published annually by the Receiver General for Canada and available through the Canadian Government Publishing Centre. In several volumes, it details the federal government's spending habits.

Public Accounts of Ontario. Published annually by the Ontario Ministry of Treasury and Economics, Toronto, in several volumes. Outlines how provincial government money is spent—from the salaries of civil servants to grants to private industry. Other provinces have similar books.

The Ontario Government Structure and Functions. By George G. Bell and Andrew D. Pascoe; published by Wall & Thompson of Toronto, 1988. Provides a good overview of how the different components of the Ontario government operate.

The Public Sector. Published weekly by Southam Communications Ltd., as a newsletter. Provides analysis of federal and provincial policies, pending legislation and new laws.

Report of the Auditor General of Canada to the House of Commons. Published by the Auditor General of Canada. Available from the Canadian Government Publishing Centre. Criticizes government spending where appropriate.

Using the Access to Information Act. Written by two gifted lawyers, Heather Mitchell and Murray Rankin; published by International Self-Counsel Press, Vancouver, 1984. If you plan to use freedom of information laws in this country, you must read this book.

You and Your Local Government. By C.R. Tindal, published by the Ontario Municipal Management Development Board, Oshawa, 1988. Focuses on Ontario, but an excellent primer on the ways in which local governments function.

LABOUR

Collective Bargaining Information Sources. Published by Labour Canada. An invaluable reference guide to the many kinds of information available for collective bargaining and other industrial relations purposes in Canada. Lists practically every source in Canada with addresses and telephone numbers; updated regularly. Available free to anyone involved in industrial relations.

Corporations and Labour Unions Returns Act. Published annually by Statistics Canada, Ottwa, in two volumes. Includes a lot of useful data on national and international unions operating in Canada.

Directory of Labour Organizations in Canada. Published each year by Labour Canada. Provides information on national and international unions as well as independent labour organizations. A good guide for looking up addresses and acquiring quick statistics.

The Current Industrial Relations Scene in Canada. Edited each year by Mary Lou Coates, David Aerosmith, and Pradeep Kumar; published by the Industrial Relations Centre, Queen's University, Kingston, Ontario. An important reference book for anyone involved in industrial relations. Provides analysis and statistics.

LAW

The Canadian Law Dictionary. Published by the Law and Business Publications (Canada), Toronto, 1980. One of many useful dictionaries that specialize in defining legal terms.

Canada Law List. Published annually by the Canada Law Book, Aurora, Ontario. A mammoth book listing the addresses of government and other sources relating to legal issues, including courts.

Courts and the Media. By Stuart M. Robertson; published by Butterworths, Scarborough, Ontario, 1981. An excellent book that unravels the court process in Canada. Chapter four is especially helpful in clarifying what access is allowed to some court records.

Criminal Procedure in Canada. By P. Michael Bolton; published by International Self-Counsel Press, Vancouver. An excellent source book for understanding the criminal justice system in Canada.

Latin Words and Phrases for Lawyers. Published by Law and Business Publications (Canada), 1980. Translations of significant Latin words, phrases, and maxims used by the legal profession. Very useful in interpreting legal documents.

Law and the Media: A Reporter's Guide To Canada's Criminal Justice System. By Harold J. Levy; published by the Canadian Bar Foundation in Ottawa, 1986. Required reading for anyone wanting to learn about Canadian courts. A very significant book.

Legal Research Handbook. By Douglass T. MacEllven; published by Butterworths, 1986. Provides an overview of sources including computer data available for legal research in Canada. It also shows how to use these sources.

The Law and the Media. By Clare F. Beckton; published by The Carswell Company, Agincourt, Ontario, 1982. The first chapter is an excellent overview of Canada's legal system and court structure.

RESEARCH

Asking Questions: The Art of the Media Interview. By Paul McLaughlin; published by International Self-Counsel Press, 1988. A great book for improving your interviewing techniques.

Indian History and Claims: A Research Handbook. By Bennett Ellen McCardle; published by the department of Indian and Northern Affairs Canada, Treaties and Historical Research Centre, 1982. This obscure two-volume set is well worth looking at to discover interesting research methods and sources.

Research: A Practical Guide to Finding Information. By Peter Fenner and Martha A. Armstrong; published by William Kaufmann, Los Altos, CA, 1981. Good advice on how to use libraries to obtain information on science and technology.

The Man From the Cave. By Colin Fletcher; published by Alfred A. Knopf, Inc., 1981. A fascinating book in which the author explains how he found a trunk in a cave and spent the next ten years researching it. The techniques and sources used in the research are revealing. Highly worth reading.

The Reporter's Handbook: An Investigator's Guide to Documents and Techniques. Edited by John Ullmann and Steve Honeyman; published by St. Martin's Press, New York, N.Y., 1983. Excellent for exploring techniques of research and sources available on a multitude of subjects in the U.S.

Where to Go for What: How to Research, Organize, and Present Your Ideas. By Mara Miller; published by Prentice-Hall, Englewood Cliffs, N.J., 1981. Extremely well-written and interesting; explores the techniques of research. Worthwhile, even though the references are limited to American sources.

Winning by Telephone. By Gary S. Goodman; published by Prentice-Hall Canada, Scarborough, Ontario, 1982. Recommended reading if you want to learn how to use the telephone effectively. One of several books by Goodman on this subject.

TRACING PEOPLE

Catalogue of Directories Published and Areas Covered by Members of International Association of Cross Reference Directory Publishers. Published by Cole Publications, Lincoln, Nebr. This booklet provides a substantial list of the city directories available across North America, along with their publishers' names and addresses. Doesn't list all city directories, but is quite comprehensive. (City directories are compiled in a variety of ways and may contain a great deal of information on people, including occupation, address, how long the person has had a particular telephone number, and much more. They are often used for tracing people or for marketing products.)

Tracing Your Ancestors in Canada. Available through the Manuscript Division of the Public Archives of Canada. Call (613) 996-7458 for a free copy.

GENERAL REFERENCE

A Dictionary of Acronyms and Abbreviations in Library and Information Science. Compiled by R. Tayyeb and K. Chandna; published by the Canadian Library Association, Ottawa, 1985. A good example of just how specialized dictionaries have become.

Amnesty International Report. Published by Amnesty International Publications, London, England. Appears every year and documents abuses of human rights around the world.

Association of Canadian Publishers. Published annually by the Toronto-based Association of Canadian Publishers. Available free of charge.

Association of Consulting Engineers of Canada. Published by that organization (based in Ottawa), on an ongoing basis. Lists consulting engineers and their area of expertise.

Canada Year Book. Published annually by the federal Minister of Supply and Services, Ottawa. Provides a wide range of data on the economic, social, and political life of Canada.

Canadian Almanac and Directory. Edited by Susan Bracken; published annually by Copp Clark Pitman, Toronto. Includes names and address of key officials and departments at all levels of government, a long list of associations, and other useful information.

Canadian Business Index. Published monthly by Micromedia Limited, Toronto, with a cumulative index at the end of each year. Includes about 200 major business publications in Canada. An invaluable reference tool.

The Canadian Encyclopedia. Published in four volumes in 1988 by Hurtig, Edmonton. Contains thousands of pages of useful information on all aspects of Canada with thousands of biographies. Of use to anyone doing any kind of research on Canada.

Canadian Library Yearbook. Published each year by Micromedia Limited and lists public, college, university, government, and special libraries in Canada.

Canadian Medical Directory. Published annually by Southam Communications, Don Mills, Ontario. Lists doctors by province and town, as well as all hospitals in Canada.

Canadian News Index. Published monthly by Micromedia Limited with a cumulative index at the end of each year. Indexes seven of the country's major newspapers by subject and name. Invaluable for any researcher.

Canadian Reference Sources. By Dorothy Ryder; published by the Ottawa-based Canadian Library Association in 1981. The information in this text was updated in the article, "Canadian Reference Books; Or Benevolent Ignorance Dispelled," by Edith T. Jarvi and Diane Henderson, which appeared in the *Reference Services Review*, Volume 2, Fall 1983, pp. 87 to 95 with bibliography.

Canadian Who's Who. Published annually by University of Toronto Press; profiles notable Canadians.

Directory of Associations in Canada. Edited by Brian Land and Liba Berry; published once a year by Micromedia Limited. Invaluable for locating organizations and experts of any kind. Lists 16,500 associations in the 1988 edition, each of which has been indexed under 1200 subject classifications, and the serials of each association.

Engineering, Science & Computer Jobs. Published annually by Peterson's Guides Inc., Princeton, New Jersey. Profiles companies which offer engineering, science or computer jobs in the U.S. and, to a lesser extent, in Canada. Provides basic data such as company location, salaries, benefits, and other information.

Guide to Basic Reference Materials for Canadian Libraries. Edited by Claire England and others; published by the University of Toronto Press periodically.

Lesko's New Tech Sourcebook: A Directory to Finding Answers in Today's Technology-Oriented World. By Matthew Lesko; published by Harper & Row, 1986. Lesko's various best-selling books are aimed at the U.S. market and are recommended to any researcher who needs American government information.

Oxbridge Directory of Newsletters. Published by Oxbridge Communications, Inc., New York, N.Y. An incredibly valuable guide to newsletters in the U.S. and Canada; can help anyone locate experts quickly on any topic. A fascinating book.

Sources: The Directory of Contacts for Editors, Reporters and Researchers. Published twice-yearly by Toronto's Barry Zwicker. An invaluable reference tool for locating experts in every field. Contains a handy subject index. Provides a brief description of 1094 informative organizations and Parliamentary names and numbers. To order a copy call (416) 964-7799.

Theses in Canada: A Bibliographic Guide. By Denis Robitaille; one of several excellent sources published by the Canadian Library Association to track Canadian theses.

Ulrich's International Periodicals Directory. Published annually by R.R. Bowker, New York, N.Y. (A quarterly publication, *Ulrich's Quarterly*, brings the Directory up to date.) Provides a list of all major publications and states which have been indexed and where. Saves researchers a lot of unnecessary wading through back issues of publications because it alerts them to the fact that an index exists. (A similar publication is the *Standard Periodical Directory*.)

Who Knows What: Canadian Library-Related Expertise. Published by the Canadian Library Association; compiled by award-winning librarian Susan Klement. A directory for anyone requiring library-related sevices.

800 Service Directory. Published by Telecom Canada, Ottawa; provides toll free numbers of every description across Canada. You can order a copy by calling 1-800-561-6600.

Index

CREDITS

Grateful acknowledgement is made to the following business organizations and government departments for permission to reprint copyrighted material. Every effort has been made to trace copyright holders, and any errors or omissions drawn to the publisher's attention will be rectified in subsequent editions.

Figures 12.1, 12.2, 12.3, 12.4, and 12.5: Micromedia Limited, Toronto, Ontario.

Figure 13.1: Department of Buildings & Inspections, City of Toronto.

Figure 13.2: Committee of Adjustment, City of Toronto.

Figure 15.1: Corporations Branch, Department of Consumer and Corporate Affairs. Reproduced by permission of the Minister of Supply and Services Canada.

Figure 15.2: Statistics Canada.

Figures 15.3 and 15.4: Treasury Board. Reproduced by permission of the Minister of Supply and Services Canada.

NOTES

NOTES

NOTES

NOTES

NOTES